The Healing Power of Love

Creating Peace in Marriage and Family Life

John and Kathleen Colligan

Paulist Press • New York • Mahwah

Cover illustration by William Mihalko.

Library of Congress Cataloging-in-Publication Data

Colligan, John,
The healing power of love / by John and Kathleen Colligan.
p. cm.
ISBN 0-8091-2967-1 (pbk.)
1. Christian life—Catholic authors. 2. Love—Religious aspects—Christianity. 3. Peace—Religious aspects—Christianity. 4. Colligan, John. 5. Colligan, Kathy. I. Colligan, Kathy.
II. Title.
BX2350.2.C6125 1988
248.4′82—dc19 88-2389
CIP

Published by Paulist Press
997 Macarthur Blvd.
Mahwah, N.J. 07430

Printed and bound in the United States of America

Contents

DEDICATION

To
Fr. Charles A. Gallagher, S.J.
who has a vision for what the Sacrament of Matrimony can be for the church, and challenges us to live it.

Foreword

It is my conviction that one of our great weaknesses in the Catholic Church is that we don't use the full powers of the Sacraments of Baptism and Confirmation. We tend to look on our membership in the Church in terms of being passive recipients of the good things that the Church has to offer. We've pretty much restricted those good things to Sunday Mass and to special occasions like the Baptism, First Communion, First Confession, and Confirmation of our children. We don't really allow the Lord to affect us in our daily lives.

Hurting is part of the human condition. Most of the hurts that come into people's lives are little ones, although the cumulative effect of those can sometimes be devasting. But all of us, at least sometime in our lives, experience major hurts. The only recourse we have in American society today is to turn to the professional counselor. Counseling is a wonderful gift from God. It comes out of the intellectual powers that He has given us. But counseling can only put us into a condition where we can cope with our hurts. It doesn't actually remove the hurts and make us fully whole again. That takes divine intervention. Such divine action is part of the power of the Sacraments, especially Confirmation. In addition, each of us has the power to heal in the name of the Lord Himself.

There are many ways to heal. Very frequently we restrict it just to one type of healing, the charismatic form, which is very good and praiseworthy. It certainly should be utilized. But there are many forms of healing in the Church. We can never thank our charismatic brothers and sisters enough for having raised our consciousness about the possibility of healing. However, we cannot limit ourselves and, worse, limit the Lord to just one way of making His people whole again.

John and Kathy Colligan describe in this book the ways that they have experienced healing one another, calling upon their sacramental powers of Confirmation focused through the prism of their Sacrament of Matrimony.

While few families have experienced the trials that the Colligans have endured, every family has some trials or difficulties. These cause them to wonder about themselves, who they are and why God permits such suffering. When we reflect on how this family responds to suffering, we get insights into lay spirituality. In this book I believe the Church is gifted with an outstanding modern example of how a married couple calls upon the grace of their sacrament and the prayerful support of the Body of Christ to guide them through their suffering and into a heightened awareness of the joy of the Kingdom of God.

One danger in reading this book is to focus on the trauma that the Colligans experienced. The point is not to concentrate on what happened to them and how terrible it was, but to concentrate on how they handled that trauma, how they responded to one another, and to the Lord's presence in their midst. We should focus on how they really made each other new again in the Lord. Their story calls us to focus on those close to us. It shows us how we can reach out in love and in the power of grace. Everyone has a story of faith to tell, a personal journey of God's presence in their lives—sometimes in joy and other times in sorrow. We continue to live Scripture in our days with a devoted God who walks with us.

This book tells the story of how one family's faith journey was profoundly influenced by their prayerfulness, their experience of Scripture, their sacramental way of life and their joining with other members of the Body of Christ. It offers many practical examples for down-to-earth, flesh-and-blood spiritual growth which will help anyone who walks in the same path. Of course, this book doesn't have all the answers, but it is an exciting record of one family's observations and insights as they grew in their faith.

Chuck Gallagher, S. J.

Introduction

When we reflect on our personal experiences of life in our families we all know that things don't always turn out the way we expected them to. When problems strike our families we normally react by trying to keep it quiet, handle it ourselves, and make believe everything is okay. Sometimes the problems are overwhelming and we find ourselves out of control, filled with fear, anxious and hopeless. That is where we found ourselves a few years ago. It was a living hell and, begging God's mercy, we turned to prayer and to our faith family for support to pull us through.

We were an ordinary couple living an ordinary life with our three teenaged children: Kathleen Jr. (Casey), John, and Anne. As a couple, we had experienced Marriage Encounter and Charismatic Renewal. We were on a spiritual journey; we knew it and welcomed it. We longed to do God's will in our lives and to bring His love to others. Responding to an admonishment in scripture to care for the widow and the orphan that we sensed was meant for us, we adopted two children to add to our family. They were a brother and sister, aged 10 and 13 at the time.

From the beginning, it was a very difficult placement for both us and the adopted children. Coming from nine years of foster care and abuse and neglect in their own home, they were working out problems and frustrations that even they couldn't identify. On our part, we were trying to cajole and encourage, love and enrich, two children who neither loved us nor trusted us. We couldn't believe they could resist our invitation to belong fully to us even though they often told us they weren't sure they wanted to.

We were good people wanting to do good things and follow the teachings of Jesus in our daily lives. Yet, in a two year period we experienced the following events in our family:

- Our son, John, informed us that his girlfriend was pregnant. He was 19 and she was 18; both in college.
- They were married and three months later their baby was born, our first grandchild. Elizabeth was born with severe Spina-Bifida. In spite of life-saving surgery and our best efforts and many prayers, she died when she was six weeks old.
- Four months later our adopted son, Brian, ran away from home at the age of 17 and continued to break into our house whenever we were away, for the next six months.
- While this was going on, John and his wife lost a second child in a miscarriage. They began to experience difficulties in their marriage after that.
- A few months later, our adopted daughter, Andrea, overdosed on drugs and alcohol and swore she would kill herself if she ever had to live with us again. The county eventually assumed responsibility for her and she was sent to a school for troubled girls.
- Simultaneously, our son and his wife separated. He was deeply depressed, working several jobs, going to college and his life was in a shambles. It broke our hearts to see how sad he was.
- We were going to Colorado and invited him to go with us for the six week stay. There we watched him heal and come to life again. We began to have hope. He got a job in Denver and decided to stay.
- Three weeks after we returned home, he was murdered.

Life is not always fun or easy. Sometimes it's nearly impossible in its turbulence and complexities. As we lived through these times, we often reflected on scripture and the teachings of the church on how we ought to live. As we thought about the story of the Prodigal Son, we recalled how the father was standing in the roadway, waiting for the return of his child. After Brian ran away and we were able to locate where he was living, we were less concerned about his safety. We too found ourselves keeping a watch for our son. Only we were saying, "If I can get my hands on that kid, I'll squeeze his neck until his eyes pop out." Hardly a scriptural response, but definitely the response of parents without inner peace.

When we went on retreat after our granddaughter died, we went to the chapel to pray. At the time of the baby's birth and throughout her short life and death, we thought we had handled everything beautifully—even nobly. We were, after all, believers. Yet, looking up at the crucifix in the chapel at the retreat house, Kathy could only grit her teeth and say, "I don't want to pray to You. I am so angry right now, I want to scream, not pray."

As we waited in the Emergency Room of the hospital while they examined our daughter, Andrea, we could hear her screaming at the nurses how much she hated us and how we abused her. Sometimes one of them would walk by and scowl in our direction. Then we would recall, " . . . My yoke is easy and my burden light."(Mt. 11:30) And we could only ask, "If Your yoke is easy and Your burden light, then what are we doing wrong? Are we doing Your will or not? Aren't we good people? Aren't we trying to do as You ask? Then why does it turn out like this, Lord? Is Jesus a liar? Did He really mean what He said, or not?"

When Johnny was killed, we could only wonder why. He was a light in our life and a child of joy. "Why, Lord, does he have to end this way, alone on a hillside? Is this the reward You promise Your people, the comfort You offer? Where are You now, when we need You? Where were You when he needed You?"

Sometimes God seems silent, and we walk alone. Sometimes, even in the good times, His advice sounds nice, but doesn't always seem to go along with common sense. "Do not worry about what you are to eat or what you are to put on . . . "

"Lord, we're supporting five kids and they're all in Catholic schools. We have to pay for books and tuition, and we have to keep them decently clothed. On top of that we have all sorts of counseling expenses for our adopted kids and demands for transportation and housing. How can we not worry about how we're to care for ourselves. We live in America, Lord, and we and our children are used to the American way of life. We live in a land of bounty and comfort, and we want it all—with You there to help us."

The dilemma we face is, how do we live out scripture in our daily lives? How can we take the Word of God and make it personal? If we do, will God always bless us in the way we think He should? For us personally, we had to know: How can we love children who reject us? What is our response to be to their hostility and hatred? How can we let go of our anger, our resentment, and our frustration with the circumstances of our lives? How can we be healed of our son's death? How can we find peace?

This book describes how one couple sought and obtained inner peace. In it, we tell something of our own story. It also includes our observations about the tensions that arise in interpersonal relationships and observations about how we handle these tensions. Finally it includes suggestions for how you might find peace in your own life even in the midst of turmoil and confusion.

Throughout the book we have inserted prayers or exercises meant to help you in your own search for inner peace. You will find that in the exercises we have alternately used the pronouns "he" or "she." We did this to be inclusive of all of us rather than exclusive. All of the behavior described could belong to any of us, male or female.

Our book is meant for ordinary people—people like ourselves who are searching for some meaning in their lives and are turning to God for the answers. As we tell our story, we ask you to focus not on us, but on yourself and the story of your family. How has God called you to love one another? Who is there in your life whom you should forgive or with whom you should reconcile? How is God speaking to you today? Everyone has a story to tell. What is the story of your faith journey with the Lord?

1

Working Toward Peace

"They shall beat their swords into plowshares . . . " (Mi. 4:3). This passage from scripture is often associated with the peace movement. We usually think of working for peace in terms of nuclear disarmament, cutting back on defense spending, witnessing for peace, etc.

We believe that while we must bring peace to our world, we must also bring peace to our homes. Peace must begin within our own sphere of influence. Most war-like behavior comes to us personally from those within our own families and our own communities. No one can get to us like the people who know us and love us best. No one can cause so much pain or havoc in our lives as those whom we expect to love us.

Most of our own hostile behavior is directed at the members of our family. We seem to save our worst for one another. Maybe it's because we take them for granted and assume they have to love us. Maybe it's because they have hurt us and we're trying to get even. Maybe we're simply exhausted and have nothing left to give each other.

Within the family we find the core of our love, our life and our expectations for what life ought to be. We can quit our jobs, move away from our neighborhood, drop out of school, break off friendships and resign from organizations when we get to the point where we can't stand to be there anymore. They are all temporary commitments.

The family is different. We can leave home, move to the opposite coast or half-way around the world. We can change our name and deny that we ever knew one another, but we can't really run away from our family. For better or worse, they have their fingerprints all over us. They have formed us, molded us and told us, "This is who you are. This is what we think of you." Somehow we have to make peace with our family if we are to have peace within ourselves.

All of us long for inner peace, but we live in a time when few have real peace. Most of us blame our lack of inner peace on external factors, so we try to manipulate the circumstances in our lives in order to achieve peace. Many people would define inner peace as a state where they would experience no stress, where life would have at least a certain amount of order to it, where they could depend on others not to hassle them, and where they might have the freedom to do what they really want.

According to this definition, many have reduced stress in their lives. They have achieved order and discipline and have found instead: boredom, and monotony. They have reduced the number of people in their lives by moving away, or through divorce or by limiting the number of children they will have and have found not peace, but loneliness.

How many people long for early retirement and release from jobs they can barely tolerate? How many more are afraid to retire because they have no place to go, nothing to do, and no one they wish to be with—especially their spouse? While a self-centered lifestyle based on gratifying immediate needs may fill short term wishes, it can prove to be counterproductive in the long run.

Many have accepted the belief that at age 18 or 21, children should leave home. Adult children who choose to remain at home frequently find themselves treated as unwelcome tenants. In our society, it's often considered unhealthy or abnormal for adult children to remain home with their parents. So we have many small households set up across the country. We have preserved our independence and the right to make our own decisions without consulting one another. We have lost our sense of unity, and of common purpose. We no longer have to share what we own, but we have to work harder to obtain our own things. We have less freedom, not more.

Almost 50% of married couples free themselves from the pressure and hassle of a marital relationship at some point in their lives. Seeking the freedom and independence they believe is awaiting them in the singles' world, they choose the lonely and often frightening path of divorce. In some cases, divorce may be the only acceptable outcome to a life characterized by abuse or degradation. In other cases, the apparent freedom that was so attractive, turns out to be a different form of servitude. The couple now no longer has to submit to one another, but they find society has its own rules that demand their submission. Moving into the singles' dating scene, being a Sunday father, or working and raising a family alone can be a desperately lonely way to live.

We do not believe that inner peace is achieved on a long term basis merely by changing the exterior circumstances of our lives. Changing jobs, moving away from family, breaking up our homes, or retiring early may bring a quick fix that feels good for a short while, but achieves few lasting results. One of our daughters commented a few years ago, "When things are going well, I can live anywhere. When things aren't going well, I need family."

The key to inner peace is letting go of all those things we are hanging onto, and putting them in God's hands. We are told the three things that make the world go around are power, sex, and money. So they are among the first things we have to let go. Our experience is that we also had to let go of much of what we hold dearest about ourselves: our good reputation, our strong sense of responsibility, our desire to be perfect. We also had to let go of our children and our desire to mold them in our image.

We believe the main reason why most of us can't let go is because of our poor self-image. We have an image of ourselves that is often false, and we are trying to live up to what we think we should be. Most of us have been hurt in our lives also, and we are trying to compensate. If we can be healed of our poor self-images and of our hurts, especially our biggest hurts, we can let go of many of the other things which are really only added baggage in our lives. Then we can be truly free—free to be who we are called to be by God. He has made us in His image. Do we really believe that?

We would define inner peace as a state where one is "resting in the Lord." Here, a person feels at home with himself. He does not fret about, or try to change, those things he cannot control. The person with inner peace does not need to manipulate or maneuver others to achieve her will. She is able to accept the fact that she is not the Messiah; Jesus is. Therefore, the peaceful person lets God be God. This person has an implicit trust in the Lord that combines the confidence of the child with the wisdom of the adult. St. Francis of Assisi is a model to us of a person of inner peace.

The exterior circumstances of the life of the peace-filled person may or may not be filled with turbulence. Certainly, this person does not run away from life or loved ones. But the response of this person to stress is different from that of other people. This person brings to all situations serenity and good judgment. That is the gift of counsel. The gifts of the Holy Spirit are fully active in this person and there is a simplicity and joy in life that goes beyond measure and beyond words.

In order to achieve inner peace, we must begin not outside ourselves, in the circumstances of our lives, but inside ourselves, where all the turmoil and confusion lives. In order to bring true peace to our families, the church, and the world, we must first know inner peace. We must begin within.

2

The Beginning

We have always assumed that as a family, we belong to one another. We have made a lifelong commitment to one another in Matrimony and, together, we have made a commitment to love our children and be part of their lives and the lives of their children as long as we are able. We have also assumed a certain responsibility for our parents and our aging relatives. They are ours, and more and more, as they get older, they have come to depend on us for help and support. We also have an extended family of brothers and sisters, nieces and nephews, aunts and uncles to whom we feel a close bond. While we may not see one another often, we talk on the phone frequently, and share mutual concern for one another and other family members.

If one of the characteristics of family is commitment, then certainly another is love. We are called to love one another. "If anyone says, "My love is fixed on God," yet hates his brother, he is a liar." (1 Jn. 4:20)

Until recently, we didn't take this passage too literally—we knew that the brother referred to was our neighbor, our fellow parishioner, the person on the other side of town or the other side of the world whom we are called to love. If we are called to love the stranger however, and think of the stranger as brother or sister, then how much more we are called to love the brother or sister in our own family—even the brother or sister who has abused us, can't stand us, or thinks we're jerks. We are to love even the brother or sister we detest . . . the one we hope won't show up at the family reunion . . . the one we'll be sure to avoid as much as possible if she does show up.

We believe that ultimately, we ourselves will be judged not

on our worldly accomplishments, our college degrees, the amount of money we have earned, whether or not we own our own home or sent our children to graduate school. We believe the only question asked will be, "How well did you love one another—most especially those whom I sent to be closest to you?"

For many years we based our lives on being achievers, and we were reasonably successful. The peak of our success came after 14 years of marriage when on the same day John got his Ph.D. and Kathy got her B.A. We had spent the preceding two years literally working night and day so we could maintain our full-time jobs and raise our three children. There we stood with the ink still wet on our college degrees for which we had sacrificed so much. It was to have been one of the most joyful days of our lives. We thought we would feel fulfilled; instead we were both filled with an overwhelming sadness.

For years we had tried to figure out God's plan for our lives. We frequently commented that we would love to find a white-haired old wise man to whom we could turn for counsel. The wizard never showed up so we chose as our motto, "Don't just stand there, do something!" We followed the world's wisdom and filled our lives with activities and set goals for our own achievements and those of our children.

For a long time we were so busy birthing and raising our three children, building our careers, and establishing ourselves as good citizens in our community, we didn't stop to reflect on where our lives were headed. By the time that long sought-after graduation day arrived, we were tired and disappointed. Suddenly we realized that we had been in such hot pursuit of success in the world's terms that we had put all of our effort into *doing* rather than *being*. Separately we discovered a deep loneliness and emptiness in ourselves. The question, "Is this what life is all about?" haunted us. We wondered, "Why did God make us? What is our purpose in life? Is this all there is?" The emptiness of a life based on achievement and personal fulfillment was oppressive.

We had a burning thirst for a return to the closeness and love with which our marriage had begun, but we had no idea how to do that. We decided we needed to get away for awhile—just the two of us. We began to save for a winter cruise to some sunny place. It so happened that Marriage Encounter was starting up in our area and before we could take our cruise, some friends twisted our arms to go on a weekend retreat.

> **K**: *I was hoping to change John on that weekend. I was nineteen years old when we got married in 1958—still a girl in my attitudes and outlook on life. Now I was a woman of 33. Women's Lib had hit me in full force. As I had read The Feminine Mystique, I knew without a doubt, I was married to a male chauvinist. I kept thinking, "This man I married 14 years ago doesn't even know me anymore. He still thinks I'm a little girl." I wanted John to change and be more like me—understanding, caring and sensitive. I was certain that if he would change, I could have a happy marriage.*

> **J**: *I went on the Marriage Encounter Weekend just to get our friends off my back. I honestly didn't expect anything from the weekend and couldn't imagine what Kathy and I could possibly find to say to one another that would consume 72 hours I expected to be bored so I took along a New York Times so I'd have some reading material handy for dull moments.*

God is a surprise! He reached into our hearts on that weekend and welcomed us back to Him. We were emptied out and filled with the spirit of Jesus Christ. Loneliness, sadness, uncertainty, and anxiety were replaced with inner peace. We had learned a new language—the language of feelings. When we began to communicate our feelings to one another rather than just our thoughts and opinions, we began to break through the protective barriers we had placed around ourselves to shield us from one another. We began to listen, to understand and to accept each other. We learned that we both had to change.

It was at this time that we also met Fr. Chuck Gallagher. We were attending a Marriage Encounter workshop and over a casual lunch began telling him about our children. We were proud parents and bragged about their good grades, their successes in sports and school activities, their trophies and accomplishments. "They sound like great kids," he said, "really great achievers."

"They are," we replied with big proud smiles. "These kids will go far. They're definitely college material. Our only concern is in raising our daughters. How can we train bright, capable young women to go to college and have a career and still be satisfied to be wives and mothers? Is it even possible to be a career woman and the mother of a large family?" We doubted it.

"Don't teach your children to be achievers," he told us. "Teach them to be lovers." He pointed out that their trophies would soon gather dust on the shelf and many of their achievements and awards would fade. What would be lasting in their lives would be love. If we could teach them to love, they would be prepared to enter into marriage, the priesthood, or religious life. Or they might remain as singles in the church. Whatever they chose to do, however, they would do it in a spirit of love and caring for others. They would eventually make their decisions in life based on love, not achievement and personal fulfillment.

We had never heard anything so simple, yet radical. But the more we discussed it, the more it sounded like a good idea. We couldn't figure out how to teach our children to be lovers though. We knew how to encourage them in school and in sports. How do you teach a child to love?

"It's simple," Fr. Chuck replied, "by example! Teach them by your own example." Now he had a big grin on his face.

We were thunderstruck. The only way to do that was to change ourselves.

We always think of this time as the beginning of our letting go of our frantic search for inner peace through our achievements. Ever since that time, we consciously try to make our own relationship and our relationship with God our priority. After that came our relationship with our children and then our extended family. Then came our commitment to others, our involvement in church, school and finally civic activities.

We no longer measured our own success in life in terms of how much we earned, what titles we had, nor in what we owned. Nor did we measure our children that way. The quality of our relationships was more important than any worldly recognition. We only had to work on these relationships and really communicate with one another to make them great.

As a couple and as parents we knew for certain that love was more important than our accomplishments. We knew that God had sent us specifically to each other and called us to be a family. We knew also that this sort of deep and lasting life together takes time and energy.

3

Getting In Touch With Each Other

The best way to work on our relationship is to open our lines of communication with each other. It was at a Marriage Encounter Weekend that we got in touch with our feelings and began to share on a much deeper level with one another. A feeling is an emotion that arises spontaneously within us. Our strongest feelings are usually easy to identify. They are often in response to a person or a situation in which we find ourselves. For example:

- My boss criticized me at work. I feel humiliated and angry.
- My child misbehaves in public. I feel embarrassed and frustrated.
- My husband kisses me and tells me he loves me. I feel pleased and content.

Another way to identify a feeling is to substitute the words, "I am . . . " for "I feel . . . " Thus we have, "I am humiliated and angry." "I am embarrassed and frustrated." "I am pleased and content."

Sometimes our feelings seem to come out of nowhere. For example: We may wake up feeling irritable and hostile. On another day, we may wake up feeling exceptionally bright and good about the day.

The same situation may not always cause the same feelings in us. For example: Heavy, slow traffic might not bother us one day. We can be very calm and relaxed about the whole situation. On another day, the same situation makes us feel hostile and aggressive. We might silently curse the slow driver or ourselves for starting too late. Upon reflection, we may realize we're actually angry with ourselves.

Some days the noise and nonsense of our children doesn't bother us at all.

K: *I remember sitting in our kitchen with my mother one day while our children played in the next room. "How can you stand all that noise?" she asked.*

"What noise?" I inquired. I was honestly baffled by her question; I had become so accustomed to hearing the children at play. On other days however, their noise and games would be very grating on my nerves, and I'd quickly send them outside so I could find some peace and quiet.

There are all types of words used to describe feelings. Some describe pleasurable feelings like: joy, excitement, enthusiasm, happiness, hope. It's these feelings we wish would stay forever. Other words describe unpleasant feelings like: jealousy, anger, fear, irritability, anxiety, resentment. We'd like these feelings to go away. Sometimes we're even ashamed to have them.

Feelings in themselves are neither right nor wrong. They have no moral value. However, the way we choose to express our feelings has definite moral connotation attached to it.

J: *If I'm irritable in the morning, that's not wrong. If I take out my irritation on my family, shouting at the children, cursing Kathy, or ignoring them altogether, there can be a moral judgment about my behavior.*

We can accept our feelings. We don't have to deny we feel irritable or pretend we're not. But we don't have to accept the crummy behavior that may accompany our negative feelings. Even while we acknowledge that this is not a good morning for us, we can act in a loving way with others. We may lack our usual warmth or enthusiasm behind our actions, but that's still better than destroying other people through our verbal or non-verbal abuse.

We learned that when we understood our feelings, we accepted a major part of who we really are. Our thoughts, opinions and judgments reflect our attitudes and ideas. They may be right or wrong, correct or incorrect. While we could argue with one another about our opinions, we learned we couldn't argue about feelings.

We often used to argue about how much money we should spend at Christmas. For years Kathy had overspent, and we always started the new year heavily in debt. John would always be angry about this, seeing Kathy's behavior as irresponsible. He would always argue that Christmas was Jesus' birthday and therefore a religious holiday requiring no gifts. He was wrapped in superiority.

On her part, Kathy saw John as a selfish tightwad. She was wrapped in generosity; a subtler name for her superiority. Christmas was always a time of confrontation.

When we began to discuss the topic in terms of our feelings, Kathy spoke of her longing to bring happiness to others. She spoke of feelings of generosity and goodness—of seeing herself as a good mother. John spoke of his loneliness in the situation—of feeling frustrated and ignored. We knew we were at opposite poles in how much should be spent, but understanding and accepting each other's feelings helped us to come to a middle ground. Kathy bought much less. John helped to accommodate her need to buy gifts. He even helped shop. Christmas became a time of peace between us.

When we know and understand our own feelings, we know and understand ourselves better. When we share our feelings with those we love and trust, they learn what it's like to be us. When we share our feelings with one another, and our feelings are accepted, we are both less lonely. We can begin to build a bond of intimacy between us. The differences in our opinions matter less as we come to see one another as unique human beings, a part of the Body of Christ.

There is something in all of us that likes to blame others for the way we feel. Yet even when other people are involved, our feelings most often arise from our experiences, either past or present, and our expectations.

K: *I expected to enjoy being a wife and mother, yet after a few years, I felt trapped in the house as a housewife. Life had an endless monotony to it. Routine housework used to drive me crazy. I often told John, "A trained monkey could do what I do all day."*

I blamed John for my feelings. Sometimes I'd think, "He talked me into marrying him. I wanted to wait, but he didn't want to." Then I'd get angry with him for not helping more with the kids and for leaving every day to go to a job he enjoyed while I got stuck staying home.

John hated to listen to me talk about this. He'd get very defensive and point out that I wanted to get married and have children too. He told me that if I wanted to get out and go to work that was all right with him. Then I'd come back with, "Yes, I can work all day and still take care of the house, the children and all our meals. That's really wonderful of you to let me do that."

We were on an endless treadmill on this subject. When I stopped blaming John for the way I felt, he became free to listen. In truth, we had both chosen marriage and family. John couldn't make me feel less trapped, although he tried. He had to go to work, and I learned I didn't really want to leave the children even to earn extra money. What we could offer each other was sympathetic listening. We could discuss our feelings with each other and accept them. John told me of times he too felt trapped—like when he had a job he didn't like. But he had to keep it because he was supporting the family.

I came to understand that while motherhood wasn't quite what I had expected it to be, that wasn't John's fault. This freed John to listen without having to accept blame or solve the problem either. And as I realized I didn't really want to work at that time, I began to enjoy caring for the house and family more. When I knew I had chosen it and not gotten stuck with it, it was okay.

By sharing our common feelings and supporting and encouraging one another through difficult times, we've grown closer to one another and achieved what we both really wanted—someone who would love and understand us. We had more peace.

We also learned that feelings frequently come in layers. There are feelings under feelings.

K: *John had a work schedule that usually permitted him to come home about the same time every night. On a night when he would be late and I received no phone call from his office telling me to expect him late, I would be angry.*

I would think about how thoughtless he was and be annoyed that our dinner was getting over-cooked and dried out. Then I would start to worry about him. He usually did call; why didn't he call tonight? Maybe he had left the office and had gotten caught in traffic.

Then I'd begin to recall conversations we had just a few days before about the soft tire on the car, the weak battery, or the brakes that were slipping. There might have been an accident!

By now I'd be extremely anxious—checking the front window each time a car went by, listening for sirens, etc. If we had been cool and distant with one another lately, I'd also experience regret for not telling him I loved him more often, for assuming he'd always be there for me. I would realize again how much I loved him and wanted him home safely. Underneath the feeling of anger, was love and concern.

When he'd come in a short time later however, it wasn't love that he'd experience. It was my anger and hurt feelings that I would express. I had expected much more consideration from John, and as far as I was concerned, no meeting was so important that he couldn't call home first.

J: *I stopped calling Kathy because I knew how angry she always was when I came in late. I figured, "Why get chewed-out twice: once when I call and again when I get home? I might as well wait until I get home and only have to put up* *with it once. I appeared to be indifferent to Kathy, but I wasn't. I was annoyed with her that she didn't understand my job sometimes required these social activities, and I was frustrated in trying to explain things to her.*

When we began to understand what was going on, we were able to come to terms with the situation. When John realized how much Kathy worried about him, he decided he'd always call if it was possible. When Kathy knew she could trust John to call if he could, she decided that she always assume the best about him. She would assume he had tried to call and would be home as soon as possible. Peace reigned once more.

As a direct result of our Marriage Encounter weekend and the daily dialog that followed, we began to understand on a deeper level than ever before who we were as individuals and as a couple. As we understood ourselves and shared our feelings, a tremendous sense of confidence and trust developed within us and between us. Our self-images were improving as we experienced the deep love and respect we had for each other. We had found peace—at least in our own relationship.

At the same time, we began to experience a greater awareness of God in our lives. We began to pray together every day and attend daily Mass. We developed a strong interest in spiritual reading and often shared insights from our reading with one another. We began to read and discuss scripture together each morning at breakfast. We would take the readings for the day and talk about what we thought they meant. What was God saying to us that day? We would try to incorporate the readings into our work that day, and later would dialogue about our feelings. We also went to a Life In The Spirit seminar and received the Baptism of the Spirit.

One day we sat together at our kitchen table, held hands and prayed, "Dear Father, we love You and want to do Your will in our lives. We invite You now to be the center of our lives and our home. Help us and our family to live closer to You each day."

We had made a great beginning. We had opened-up to one

another and God, and He was gently leading us. But we still wanted to have it all—a great love relationship with each other, peace and joy in the family, and the great American way of life, and Jesus on the side. We had taken a few small steps, but we still had far to go.

4

Sexuality: Gift Or Problem?

One area we needed to look at was our sexual relationship. The way we handle our sexuality has a profound influence on our self-identity, and thus on our inner peace. The qualities of sexuality include understanding, warmth, openness to persons, compassion, and mutual support. These are among the scriptural qualities identified in Colossians:

> "Because you are God's chosen ones, holy and beloved, clothe yourselves with heartfelt mercy, with kindness, humility, meekness, and patience. Bear with one another; forgive whatever grievances you have against one another. Forgive as the Lord has forgiven you. Over all these virtues put on love, which binds the rest together and makes them perfect." (Col. 3:12–14)

Women have the unique ability to call forth these qualities from men; men have the unique ability to call them forth in women. In our own relationship, Kathy tends to be the introvert—preferring the privacy of family life to being out among people. It's usually John who moves us out beyond ourselves and our small world. On the other hand, it's Kathy who usually has the sentimental reaction to the plight of the poor, the lonely, the forgotten. It was she who first suggested, "Why don't we adopt a child?"

This transforming force within each of us, that looks at life from different points of view and calls another to share in that life, is the gift of sexuality. Human sexuality is a great reserve of energy and ambition waiting to be released. Each person must decide how to use that energy.

It can be used in a life-long commitment to celibacy such as our priests, religious brothers and sisters, and dedicated singles may choose. It can be used in a temporary commitment to celibacy until the time of marriage. It can be used in the Sacrament of Matrimony to build the Body of Christ through the procreation of children and to strengthen the relationship of the couple. All of us, regardless of our vocation, are called to chastity, i.e. spending our gift of sexuality in a manner appropriate to our vocation.

Today society is the greatest single influence on our attitudes about sex and sexuality. This was certainly true for us, just as it is for most people. Therefore it was with particular difficulty that we read in St. Paul:

> "Wives should be submissive to their husbands as if to the Lord because the husband is head of his wife just as Christ is head of his body the church, as well as its savior. As the church submits to Christ, so wives should submit to their husbands in everything.
>
> "Husbands, love your wives, as Christ loved the church. He gave himself up for her to make her holy, purifying her in the bath of water by the power of the word, to present to himself a glorious church, holy and immaculate, without stain or wrinkle or anything of that sort. Husbands should love their wives as they do their own bodies. He who loves his wife loves himself. Observe that no one ever hates his own flesh; no, he nourishes it and takes care of it as Christ cares for the church—for we are members of his body.
>
> "For this reason a man shall leave his father and mother, and shall cling to his wife, and the two shall be made into one."
>
> "This is a great foreshadowing; I mean that it refers to Christ and the Church. In any case, each one should love his wife as he loves himself, the wife for her part showing respect for her husband." (Eph. 5:22–33)

J: *I loved this passage. I thought St. Paul was really great. I read the first few verses and ignored the rest. The bible said Kathy should submit to me. I could enjoy a statement like that all my life and use it in an argument when necessary. For years I did just that!*

K: *I thought St. Paul was out of the Stone Age—probably a grumpy old bachelor who hated women. But then I began to put his passage in context. John was to love me as Christ loved the church. He was to live his whole life loving me and even give his life for me. If he could do this, could I submit to him? Submission had never even been part of my vocabulary in the past.*

As we began to communicate better, we realized how much we loved each other. As we grew in loving and confiding, trust grew also. Submission to one another and living our lives for each other has a lot to do with how well we trust the other to accept us and have reverence for who we are. We were experiencing that in our dialogue; we were ready to work on the whole area of our sexuality.

The commitment to matrimony, like the commitment to the priesthood or religious life, is one that demands not less than everything from us. Matrimony, in particular, demands the total gift of self—even to ownership of one's own body.

When we were engaged, we could hardly wait to be married so we could enjoy sexual intercourse with one another. After we were married however, it was an area in which we played a lot of psychological games.

For many years we treated our sexuality as if it were only our genital activity—an activity intended to bring personal pleasure and self-satisfaction. Of course, we were somewhat concerned about how pleasing our love-making was for the other, but essentially it was an "I-centered" activity. As such, our sexual relationship did little else than satisfy (or fail to satisfy) our personal desires of the moment. We saw it as one of the major benefits of our marital commitment but not as a part of our spirituality. Sometimes it was even the source of hurt and misunderstanding.

In every marriage, one partner has control of the sexual relationship. We used to believe this to be the person who initiated sex—the one who says, either verbally or nonverbally, "Let's make love tonight."

The person who is really in control however, is the one who has the power to say, "Yes, we will," or "No, we won't." This person has what we call, "No Power." More often than not, it is the woman who has "No Power" in the relationship.

When a person uses this power, the person is saying no to the activity. "No, I don't want to do *it*." What the other person is hearing however, is, "No. I don't want *you*, as a person." For this reason, "No Power" is very damaging to their relationship and can lead to many misunderstandings and hard feelings.

In our relationship, Kathy had "No Power." She never exactly came out and said, "No, go away," but then John never really asked, "Do you want to make love?" Instead, we had a whole set of non-verbal cues we used. If John was feeling particularly romantic when he came in from work, he'd greet Kathy with a big hug, or passionate kiss, or an extra pat on the fanny. This replaced his usual routine of a quick peck on the cheek and immediate involvement with the newspaper.

K: *If I stiffened up like a board when John hugged me, he usually got the message that tonight was not the night. Sometimes I'd anticipate John's mood and head him off with the comment, "Boy, you wouldn't believe what a terrible day I've had. I'm going straight to sleep tonight." At other times, I simply didn't feel well.*

Health wasn't the only excuse for saying no. Most of the time, in fact, I never said no at all. However, I'm a night person, while John's a morning person. When he'd head for bed by 9:30 p.m., I could easily outlast him for a few hours by staying up to watch television or read a book. I also found I could get a lot of ironing done at midnight. Then I'd tiptoe into bed, careful not to awaken John. Every now and then however, he'd surprise me, and as I slipped between the sheets, I'd hear a sultry voice, "I've been waiting for you . . . " My response was always the same, "That's not fair . . . "

In Matrimony, we are asked to belong to one another totally—to give up "No Power" with one another and make our lives a total yes to our beloved. This isn't easy because it means giving over control of our bodies and trusting the other person to be caring and sensitive. It assumes that both of us will act responsibly and lovingly.

Many good women who unquestionably love their husbands use "No Power" in their marriage because they have been deeply hurt by their husbands. When all the decisions about family planning are her problem, when the babies are hers and raising the children, and caring for the house are her job also, she is not going to be interested in giving up "No Power."

A number of years ago we decided to make our lives a total yes to one another in this area. We would make love much more often. John would learn to ask verbally, and Kathy would be the initiator more frequently. What we learned, surprised us. John began to have "headaches" at times. He didn't always feel like making love. Communications improved as we talked about our lovemaking. Kathy knew John was really listening to her and was sensitive to what she was telling him about all the responsibility she felt for the family. He began to help out more with the care of the children.

John became more affectionate. Kathy became more interested. They both knew there would not be any more frivolous excuses when John asked Kathy to make love with him. If it was necessary to say no to intercourse at one time, we decided when we would make love. We also make love in prime time—not when we were exhausted. Planning ahead, we built our day around our loving. We became more passionate.

Matrimony is a sexual sacrament, but too often even great married couples settle for living like a good brother and sister rather than passionate lovers. As a result, our children see little affection between us and come to believe what the world is telling them about how great sex is outside of marriage. We believe our children and our church need married couples who are deeply in love with each other and show it. While recognizing the private nature of love making, we think there ought to be an atmosphere in our homes that speaks of the profound love the husband and wife have for one another.

The passionate love of a man for a woman in marriage is so much more than duty, responsibility or sexual activity. It is a relationship that is total, giving, creative, committed, enthusiastic, and hopeful. Our lovemaking is a non-verbal communication of all these things and more.

Sometimes in making love, we communicate our feelings of celebration. We have just had a great day, a romantic evening, or special occasion. Then we are saying, "Wow, isn't life great! Aren't we great too!"

Sometimes we support one another. When one of us has a terrible day at work or has been the victim of criticism and complaints, our lovemaking says, "I believe in you. You are wonderful to me." When our self-image is low, and we notice the weight we've gained, the gray hair, the lines and wrinkles on our faces, we pat each other on the back and say, "You're not so bad." But our lovemaking says even more; "I think you're gorgeous and sexy. You're a real hunk. You are absolutely irresistible."

Sometimes we have made love after an argument—even when we didn't feel like it. Then our loving soothes away the left-over hard feelings, the harsh judgments, or the hidden belief, "I know I was right." We come away thinking the issue is not so important—not as long as we love each other.

Finally, our lovemaking is healing. In times of pain and deep emotional crisis, when all we want to do is curl-up in a corner and shrink away from one another, our lovemaking draws us outward into the loving reality of one another's bodies. This has certainly been true during the times of death and parting in our lives.

> **K**: *When Johnny died, all I wanted to do was to be left alone. I didn't really want anyone to touch me or come near me. But I had promised I would make love with John whenever he asked, and he asked often. As a result, he pulled me out of myself and my focus on my own pain into the warmth of his love and need for me. He literally, called me back to life.*

Sex and sexuality in God's eyes is a gift meant to be used wisely and well by His people. It is a gift that gives new life in our babies and children—and continuously brings renewed life to a relationship that is committed to being one—forever.

The relationship between a man and a woman is meant to be one of partnership in giving glory to God. The full use of the gift of sexuality takes both the head and the heart as well as the body to form a whole person and a whole church. Sexuality then, is a gift we all share to build God's Kingdom and bring His peace.

As a result of living-out this yes to each other in this area of our relationship, we have learned that we can make love even when we don't feel like it. We have become much less selfish with one another. We have also been blessed with great growth in mutual trust and sensitivity to each other's needs and desires. We are both strong, independent people. When we make love often, we find we are pre-disposed toward each other. We want to be close. When we don't make love frequently, it's easy for us to get busy and go our separate ways.

The trust we have in each other spills over into our whole relationship and helps us to assume that our partner always intends to do good in all his/her actions. This changes a normal reaction from that of angry criticism to one of compassionate understanding even when one of us does something stupid.

J: *I recall the time I spilled a cup of sticky apple cider all over the letter Kathy was writing at the kitchen table. The last thing I needed to hear was how clumsy and annoying I was. I already knew that. The last thing Kathy needed was a lecture about how she should be writing somewhere else and not in the kitchen. She had already thought of that. Instead, we didn't say a word. We simply and quietly joined together in the clean-up. Consequently, an incident that might have provoked stress and anxiety years ago, became an experience of being lovingly accepted just as we are. That builds inner peace.*

5

Sharing Our Burdens

We used to think that bad things only happened in bad families. It was common knowledge, we thought, that people from the wrong side of the tracks, people who abused drugs or alcohol, or people who lived immoral lives would have problems. In both church and society the implied promise was that if we led good lives, if we had a reasonably happy marriage and got along together, if John worked hard to provide and Kathy took good care of the home and the children, if we went to church every Sunday and generally set a good example for the kids, then everything would turn out all right. We would have a happy family and the children would grow up to be very much like us and share our values.

Experience has shown us that bad things happen to everyone, and to some people more than others. We are not always in control of our lives. We can go along and do our work and do the very best we can and still, things happen.

- Our sons can become drug users.
- Our daughters can live with their boyfriends.
- Our parents may grow into a crotchety old age.
- And we may suffer miserable health in our "golden years."

Often, we're not in control of ourselves either. While we might like to be always upbeat and full of hope, we may not really experience that. Instead, we may feel used, jealous, fearful, all the things we despise in others. While we can do some things to reasonably care for our health, we really can't know for sure if we'll have a heart attack or get cancer.

Our society idealizes the independent persons who can handle anything, hold up their head, and move on, untouched by it all. John Wayne and Rambo are our role models. No matter what happens, nothing seems to touch them. They appear to have no feelings and are incapable of being hurt. They're not real.

Those who try to live like that become plastic people, living on the surface of life—avoiding the inner reality of both their own suffering and that of those around them. They have to settle for superficial relationships so no one can get to them. This produces dispassionate, frustrated husbands and/or wives, and authoritarian priests and sisters. They may be people who live their vows, but they lack the joyous, caring enthusiasm of Jesus.

Society does not value pain, suffering, sorrow, loneliness, despair. Society certainly doesn't value a loser, much less a loser's mentality. So we cover it up, keep our problems to ourselves, and smile. Some of the circumstances we are expected to accept without missing a step are: divorce, death of a loved one, loneliness, unemployment, or family problems. How many of us have been trained to believe, "We don't hang out our dirty linen in public." When others ask us how we are, we always say, "Fine. I'm just fine." "And how's the family? How are the children?" "They're just fine too. Everything is fine."

When we began having problems with Brian and Andrea we never told anyone, not even our family. We didn't want to hear any, "I told you so's . . . " about adopting older children. We also desperately wanted Brian and Andrea to be accepted by the family. We thought if they knew of the depth of our problems, they wouldn't like the children and wouldn't want them around. We figured that whatever happened within the four walls of our house remained there. It was the way we had been raised.

When it came to Johnny's situation, things were different, but we still handled it the same way. As the parents of the unwed father we were allowed the dubious choice of whether or not we wanted to tell others about his girlfriend's pregnancy. We chose to keep it a secret. When we first got the news of the pregnancy from John in a 11:00 p.m. phone call from college, we were shocked. We were literally shaking. This was totally against everything we had taught our children about chastity before marriage. How could he do this? Hadn't we taught him to cherish and care for the person he loved? Hadn't we been clear in our teaching? Had we done enough to prepare him for life away from home?

We knew we had to tell the rest of the children and decided we should tell Kathy's mother who spent a lot of time with the family. We swore everyone to secrecy. We also confided in our pastor and another priest who was a very good friend of Johnny's. As we told them, we often cried. We acted as though there was a death in the family, not a new life. That awareness made us hesitate and begin to re-evaluate our attitudes.

As the months passed and our son returned home for summer vacation, we were almost beside ourselves. Johnny was getting counseling, but we were not. We prayed and prayed for insight, some sense of what we should do—what Johnny should do. He was tending toward marriage, but we teach marriage preparation in our parish and have seen too many bad marriages come from a hasty wedding that's meant to solve a problem. We wanted them to wait, and give it time, but it didn't look as though that would happen.

We would stay up late into the night talking about the situation. Should they marry? Should they break-up? Should the baby be placed for adoption? What if they only got married because of the baby and then something happened to the baby? They'd still be in a lifelong commitment to one another. Could they make that kind of commitment now? We looked awful and we felt awful. We weren't getting any sleep, and we were miserable.

We began to avoid people. We never stopped for coffee after Mass anymore. When people would see us in the church parking lot and ask us how we were, we'd grit our teeth, smile and wave, "Fine, everything is fine," and keep on walking.

Seven weeks had passed and we were about to go on a Family Retreat with old friends. We knew we couldn't live with people 24 hours a day for a week and convince them that everything was just great with the Colligans. Even our kids were avoiding people. We went to our friends, one by one, just before the Retreat began. We don't know what we expected—harsh judgment maybe, or criticism of us or our son—but there was none of that. Instead they wrapped their arms around us, hugged us, and shared some of their own experiences with us. We had forgotten that we weren't the first to go through this, and we were greatly relieved that we were no longer alone. We were being lifted-up by our faith family.

They all promised to pray. We were making a novena to St. Anne, asking her to intercede for us and pray for our guidance. All week long, they prayed. More than that, some of the people who were also at the camp began to come and talk. They shared with us their problems. One man burst into tears as he spoke of a homosexual son who was living out west. Another family, whom we had always considered a model family, spoke of the son who was never with them at camp. He was in prison. We began to put our problem in perspective and take our focus off ourselves and really see the problems of other good people around us.

By the fifth day of the Family Retreat, we were able to let go of the decision completely. We talked with Johnny and told him we realized we were telling him to make his own decision, but then we would always throw in an unspoken, " . . . But do it our way."

We told him we didn't know what the best thing to do was. We promised to support him completely in whatever decision he believed God called him to make. The next day he proposed to his girl and she accepted. It was the feast of St. Anne.

We learned later that Johnny had told his friends what was going on as soon as he had come home from college. They were a group of about 12 young men who had gone all through school together, and since the parochial school system is small we knew them and their parents pretty well. So Johnny asked the guys not to tell their parents about the pregnancy. He said he didn't mind people knowing about it, but his parents were deeply ashamed and keeping it a secret. He asked them to pray for guidance for him and his girl. He said he wanted to do whatever God was calling him to, but he wasn't sure what that was.

From that day on, those young men began showing up at daily Mass and often recited the rosary together for John when they were with each other. Our son knew what we didn't. No one can pray for us if they don't know we need prayer. It's true that we don't hang our dirty linen in public. There are some things we would never broadcast to a large audience. But in every parish there are at least a few good, holy people who will pray for us, and keep our requests confidential. First, however, they need to know we need prayer.

Wherever we present Workshops in parishes throughout the United States, parents come up to us and tell us how strongly they too need this kind of support in their parishes. We learned by our experience at the Family Retreat that many families have problems. Even apparently perfect families aren't always perfect. When we spoke out about our own problem, we freed them to do the same. In this way, we were able to support and encourage one another. We decided we would never keep secrets again but would always ask for help when we needed it.

When we experience trials and difficulties in our lives and we are not used to sharing, we tend to believe we are the only ones who have ever felt this way. We decide that no one else could possibly understand what it's like to go through what we're experiencing. We often withdraw and live in isolation. Yet this is not what Jesus intended for us. Independence is *not* a gospel value. Jesus called us to intimate relationships and community.

6

Searching For More

The message to "begin within" is echoed throughout sacred scripture. Proverbs is filled with advice for how one is to live. Jesus advances the Old Testament teachings and clarifies them in the New Testament. It is apparent that each of us is responsible for our own salvation, but the plan for working it out is not one of isolation and individualism. Rather, it is to be done through flesh and blood relationships.

We read in the Old Testament of the two most important commandments:

> "Therefore, you shall love the Lord, your God, with all your heart, and with all your soul, and with all your strength." (Dt. 6:5)

> " . . . You shall love your neighbor as yourself." (Lv. 19:18b)

At the Last Supper, Jesus spoke to the disciples in this way, "This is my commandment—love one another as I have loved you." (Jn. 15:12) This is an interesting extension of the commandments. Jesus did not merely repeat the second command of the Old Testàment. Nor did He say, "Love *me* as I have loved you." Instead He said, "Love *one another* . . . " He exhorted all Christians to live in the same total, close, loving relationship which He modeled. This is a powerful call to intimacy. In John 17:21, He says:

> " . . . that all may be one as you, Father, are in me, and I in you; I pray that they may be (one) in us, that the world may believe that you sent me."

We are therefore, called to build intimate loving relationships which will continuously cause the Body of Christ to become more one, not for our own sake, but for the sake of the world.

We believe the first school for practicing this call is with our family members, those God sent most intimately into our lives. This call applies to Christians throughout their entire lives, no matter what vocation they are living and no matter what age. If we do this, Jesus promised, "... All this I tell you that my joy may be yours and your joy may be complete." (Jn. 15:11) Jesus wants us to live in joy.

If we were to stand up in church on a typical Sunday morning and look out at the congregation, we would not be seeing the joy and enthusiasm of the people of the early Christian communities described in the Acts of the Apostles. Instead, we would see written on the faces of many of those gathered to celebrate: loneliness, anger, anxiety, hopelessness, boredom, indifference and pain.

Is this what Jesus meant for us? Are we to live in an endless cycle of frustration and tribulation ... or is this the Kingdom? As God's people are we to witness to despair—in which case there's little reason to follow Him—or are we to witness hope? How can we have hope in an apparently hopeless situation we can't control?

Often we have turned to prayer. In our prayer, we have asked God to fix this or change that in our lives.

> **K**: *I would often ask God to change some member of the family so that person would be easier to live with. I'd also ask Him to correct certain situations or problems we had. I had a lot of good ideas about how things ought to be. I always wanted things to turn out nice—at least nice in the way I wanted them.*

Together we prayed that God would change Brian and Andrea and make them love us and want to belong to our family. Sometimes we have prayed that God would change one of our bosses so he would appreciate us more and see our efforts. In each case, we were giving God the agenda and then asking Him to bless it and make it happen. After awhile, we began to feel pretty hopeless. Things didn't change, so we decided God didn't answer our prayers . . . or at least He didn't answer them very often. We also often found ourselves wrestling with God in prayer. When we read His words in scripture we'd think, "You don't really mean that. You're not asking that of me, are You?"

When we argued with the Lord we'd sometimes pray in a way similar to the following:

Our Father in Heaven . . .

"Are You really my Father, Lord? Do You love me as I think a Dad should love His child? If You love me, how come I don't always feel Your presence?

"Why don't I always feel special or loved and cherished? "Jesus says You want to be called our Father. I know Jesus doesn't lie. If You're my Father, what obligation does that put on both of us to know each other?

"Since You're God and You made me, You already know me. That means I have to make an effort to get to know You. That's not fair . . . it's too much work."

"Hallowed be Your name . . . "

"What's this mean? . . . A nice phrase? . . . Something I throw in to make You feel good? Why is it so important that we praise You?

"I need praise too, Lord, and nobody's looking over my shoulder telling me I'm great.

"Do You think I'm great? I suppose You do, since You tell everybody You're my Dad. Are You proud of me, Dad? Do You hallow my name in Your heart?"

"Your Kingdom come . . . "

"We live in the Kingdom. I know that. Jesus told us the Kingdom was at hand.

"How come we don't experience Your Kingdom, Lord? Why is the world so screwed up?

"I don't mean the world of nature, Lord. The seasons, the earth, the plants and animals all seem to have an inner harmony. There's an acceptance of Your will in all of nature. All that You have created sings back a tribute to You. All except us people, Lord.

"Lord, I'm not sure I want Your Kingdom to come. I'd rather build my own kingdom and give it back to You. That way I won't have to get involved in Your plans, and You can't ever accuse me of being lazy or not trying. You could ask me though, why I never listened to You."

"Your will be done . . . "

"Lord, I know You're going to love my plans. I have great ideas, and I want You to give them Your blessing.

"I want a crowd of people every night at our parish mission. I'd like a total physical healing for my friend, and I'd like a new car to replace our old one so I can get out more to help others.

"For good measure, I'd like You to work on the other members of my family. Change my mother/father and make them more agreeable. Give my son/daughter more ambition to work hard in school so they can be somebody someday. Change my husband/wife, Lord. Make him/her better; make him/her more like me.

"While You're at it, give me more power in the church too, Lord. Then I can change it to make it conform more to where I'm sure You want it to be. I have some really great ideas if other people will just step aside and let me use them."

"Give us today our daily bread . . . "

"I know You give us Yourself every day in the Eucharist, Lord, but I don't count that as my daily bread. I mean I can't really live just on the Eucharist. I need to support myself and the family. I have work to do.

"I know Jesus said, "I myself am the bread of life. No one who comes to me shall ever be hungry . . . " (Jn. 6:35), but I worry about my own hunger, Lord, and about the future too.

"I'd like to stop, to stay and talk with You awhile, but I'm in a hurry. Someday I'll have time for You. Someday I'm going to get to Mass more often, visit the Blessed Sacrament, pray every day, read scripture, go on a retreat. Someday, I'll do it all. Someday . . . "

"You see, Lord, I don't really trust You—at least I don't trust You to provide. I'm not sure You will—at least in the way I'd like.

. . . And forgive us the wrong we have done as we forgive those who wrong us . . . "

"Do You forgive me for the things I do, Lord? Lots of times I go to confession, and I don't feel forgiven. Most of the time I don't even bother with confession. I don't see a lot of what I do as really wrong anyway. If You had my mother, You'd behave the same way I do. And if You were married to the person I married . . . well, I'm only human.

"I guess I don't really have a penitential spirit, Lord. I don't really want one. It's too uncomfortable.

"And whom do I forgive? There are some people it's almost impossible to forgive.

"You tell me to love my enemies and to pray for those who persecute me. Did You really mean I should erase all my grudges? Won't people think I'm a fool? Won't they try to run all over me and use me?

"Lord, if You want me to forgive, then heal me of my fear."

"Subject us not to the trial but deliver us from evil . . . "

"Lord, when I ask to be free of trial, I mean that I don't want any troubles in my life or in the lives of my loved ones . . . no suffering . . . no sacrifices.

"I want everything to be nice, and I want everyone to be happy. I want to have a comfortable income, live in a nice home, take regular vacations, drive a dependable car and enjoy my leisure time.

"I don't want any evil. I just want to have it all, Lord. I want to live the American dream and have You on the side, for my friend and companion.

"Lord, if You can guarantee me my American middle-class way of life, I'm willing to put myself and my family in Your hands. Otherwise, I think we'd better look out for ourselves.

"You scare me, Lord. I get the feeling You want all of me and I'm not ready for that yet."

Amen.

We weren't making much progress until we began to change our prayer. We began to ask God to begin within us—to change *us* so we could live in the circumstances in which we found ourselves. Our new prayer had the following twist:

> "Lord, help me to love my husband just as he is. Help me to see his good points and focus on them. Free me from my negativity and harsh judgments about him."
>
> "Help me to love my children who aren't sure they want to belong to us. Help me love them as they are and belong to them. Even if they don't know how to be someone's children, help me never forget how to be a devoted mother or father."
>
> "Lord, help me with my job too. Send me enthusiasm for my work and contentment with my status. Give me the courage I need to go into work everyday, and help me to bring You with me into the marketplace."
>
> "Change me, Lord, to be the kind of person You want me to be. Send me the grace I need to live the life I have. Please break down any walls I have within me that keep me away from You and those You call me to love."

We were praying for God to send us His grace. Our experience is that God always answers our prayers for anything that will draw us closer to Him. And He answers our prayers immediately. So each morning as we begin the day, we identify what quality we most need that day and pray that God will send it to us. We have prayed for the gift of passion in our marriage so we will have a stronger desire for each other. We have prayed for courage to do the work that we don't feel like doing. We have asked for patience as we deal with a difficult elderly relative.

We also pray for freedom—freedom from the fear that holds us back from being all-out in our commitments to one another and to God—freedom from our self-pity that causes us to worry and fret about our lack of sleep, or our lack of free time because of all the demands on us, etc. When we have no fear and no self-pity, we find we are more patient, more compassionate, etc. We are content with the moment and the way things are. "Enough then of worrying about tomorrow. Let tomorrow take care of itself. Today has troubles enough of its own." (Mt. 6:34) Scripture was beginning to make more sense.

After many years of intellectualizing about prayer and how our lives can be affected by it, we have tried to discipline ourselves to add more prayer to our daily lives. Generally we don't "feel" anything happening to us during our prayer time; often we seem to be just going through the motions and have no sense of any change in us as a result of our prayer. But we do find that we work much more efficiently and creatively when we pray before we begin. "Wasting time" with God has become a more frequent choice for us. We have on occasion witnessed physical healings as requested in our prayer. We have experienced in ourselves and others a calm, peaceful result of our prayer. We have seen apparently impossible problems suddenly yield to acceptable solutions. Having made a small opening in our lives for God, He rushes in with love and surprises us with His gifts.

We have also developed a hunger for more prayer in our lives. We found that we couldn't find any time for quiet in our ordinary day so we started setting the alarm for an hour and a half earlier than our usual rising time. We don't get many phone calls before 7:00 a.m. In this way we can begin each day in quiet and prayer.

We find that our love relationship with God is similar to our love relationship with each other. Prayer is often routine, sometimes uplifting and magnificent—just like our relationship.

Sometimes when we talk to each other, we're very focused. We listen well and absorb the other person. At other times our mind is hop-scotching all over, and we are so distracted we hardly hear one another. That's the way our prayer is also. Some days we can meditate and really experience God's presence with us. On other days we'll spend the full time organizing our day or worrying about a problem and never seem to get anywhere. Some days we go to Mass and never hear the readings. We find ourselves going to the altar to receive the Eucharist, wondering how we could possibly have missed so much.

In our relationship, we find that sometimes it's easier to do something for others rather than spend time with them. So we'll buy a gift, fix a nice meal, plan a little surprise. At times we find it's easier to do nice things for God too, rather than spend time in prayer. We'll give an extra offering in the collection, write a letter to an old friend, or visit a sick person. Then we'll step back and say, "There it is, God. I did it all for You." Sometimes it's easier to build the tower of Babel than to sit still long enough to ask God if He wants us to do that.

Yet, just as the time we spend with one another pays off in the long run with greater understanding and deeper love in our relationship, so our time with God leads to greater understanding of Him in our lives and a much deeper appreciation of His love for us. Love grows and expands causing us to desire to change in order to please the Loved One and be closer than ever.

7

Getting Mad

We believe it's easy to be joyful with people we like or with whom we get along. When these are also the people we are related to, it's especially delightful. However, not all the people in our lives are easy to get along with. Some may be downright obnoxious. Jesus had a teaching for this also:

> To you who hear me, I say: Love your enemies, do good to those who hate you; bless those who curse you and pray for those who maltreat you. When someone slaps you on one cheek, turn and give him the other; when someone takes your coat, let him have your shirt as well. Give to all who beg from you. When a man takes what is yours, do not demand it back. Do to others what you would have them do to you. If you love those who love you, what credit is that to you? Even sinners love those who love them. If you do good to those who do good to you, how can you claim any credit? Sinners do as much. If you lend to those from whom you expect repayment, what merit is there in it for you? Even sinners lend to sinners, expecting to be repaid in full.
>
> Love your enemy and do good; lend without expecting repayment. Then will your recompense be great. You will rightly be called sons of the Most High, since he himself is good to the ungrateful and the wicked. (Lk 6:27–35)

Who is our enemy? The enemy may be in a foreign country that plots our downfall. The more real enemies, however, are those with whom we live and work. They are the people who criticize us, fail to love us, ignore us, or otherwise abuse us. These are the people who either most offend us now or have hurt us in the past. They are the ones who cause us to leave home, quit our jobs, leave our parish, and make us want to be as distant as possible.

We've all been hurt sometime in our lives. Most of us try to bury our hurts. We say things like, "Into each life a little rain must fall," or "Time heals all wounds." Good Christians speak of carrying their cross. We like to believe that our hurts haven't affected us. We are still the same loving, caring people we always were. It's just that now there are people we avoid whenever possible or certain situations that always get us upset, so we try to steer clear of them.

In essence, we become hostage to our hurts, tiptoeing through life and relationships in order to avoid getting burned again. We have no real inner peace, and therefore we cannot bring peace to others.

There is a pattern of behavior we follow when we are hurt. That pattern does not lead to inner peace but to continued misunderstanding and even sometimes to our own personal wars. The pattern includes the following general categories:

- Distancing
- Gossiping
- Forgetting
- Refusal to repent

We have found that when we get mad, we use this pattern both in our personal relationships in our family and in our parish. It goes something like this:

In the Family

Suppose John was really offended by Kathy. Maybe she did something he didn't like or failed to do something he thought she should do. For this example, let's assume that Kathy woke up in a very irritable mood and decided to be absolutely miserable to John before he went to work in the morning. She is full of nagging criticism and complaints.

1. The first thing John will do is put *distance* between himself and Kathy. If he's going out to work, he can't wait to leave the

house, and all the way there he's muttering to himself, "Boy, what a witch she turned out to be. I sure don't need that kind of treatment."

If he's staying home for a while, he makes sure that he's not anywhere near Kathy. If she's in the kitchen, he's in the living room. If she goes into the living room, he heads for the basement.

2. The next step would be for John to begin *gossiping* about Kathy. When we gossip, we find that we always go to people who will agree with us. We never gossip about someone with a person who will tell us we're off the wall or totally incorrect. So John might go to someone he works with and start out with, "You wouldn't believe what my wife did to me today . . . " He follows with a long tale of woe to anyone who will listen and sympathize. They usually respond with their own stories.

3. From there it's only a short trip to *forgetting* all about Kathy's good qualities. Soon the story is embellished with tales of not only this offense, but all the other offenses that have gone before it—even up to the time they first met. "She's always been like this—unreasonable, hostile, difficult to get along with. She's never been very nice to me." Always and never are good words to use when we're forgetting about any good qualities the other person might have. They help us lay out a lifetime of suffering and neglect.

4. The final stage is *refusal to repent*. Here, John would decide that in this case, he is a martyr. He has been unjustly treated by Kathy and he doesn't have to put up with this again. He may choose any course of action. He may decide to avoid Kathy for a few days—let her cool down. He may decide to punish her a little bit himself, stop speaking to her, be cold and distant with her, or go out with the boys for a couple of hours after work. He may decide to go a step further and stay away altogether, only going home to get his things. If it happens often enough, or the hurt is deep enough, or if John isn't deeply invested in the relationship, he may decide to get a divorce.

In the Parish

Looking at how we behave in the parish, we can see a similar pattern emerge. As our example, we could use our pastor, Fr. Pete, who is also a close personal friend. Let's say Fr. Pete does something to offend us. Maybe we came up with a great plan that we believe would totally turn the parish around and make it refreshed and renewed, and he didn't like our idea. So we're hurt and angry; he may not even be aware that he offended us.

1. The first thing we'll do is put *distance* between ourselves and Fr. Pete. If he's standing at the door greeting people after Mass, we'll use another door, or we'll slip by while he's talking to someone else. If he's coming to the same meeting, we'll avoid spending time with him and leave immediately afterward. If he's going to a church social and it's an important event for him, we may not go at all, or at least we won't go near him throughout the evening.

2. The next thing we do is *gossip*. We talk to each other first because we know we are mutually miffed. So we feed one another's anger and criticism. Then we may talk to a few other people in the parish, especially the people we know who are also not terribly happy at the moment with Fr. Pete. We make sure they hear how he has done us in and listen while they tell their own story. If some others talk to us about how great the parish is and they're thinking of joining, we make sure they know that it's not so great. It only looks that way. They may not want to join a parish with a pastor who isn't as progressive as we are.

3. The next step is for us to *forget* all about Fr. Pete's good qualities. We neglect to recall how good he has been for the parish, how he has called us together and really molded us into a community. We forget all the effort he has put into his homilies and the liturgy. We forget all the kindness he has shown us personally and the interest he has taken in us and our family. We forget about all the times he has gone out of his way to be available to us when we needed him. We only remember that in this case he doesn't share our vision—and we generalize it to the point where we know we share nothing in common.

4. Finally, we *refuse to repent*. We know we're right; he's

wrong. We mutter, "Well, that does it. He's not going to have John and Kathy to push around anymore." We may remove ourselves from active involvement in the parish. We may decide we'll fulfill our commitments, but that's all. We'll teach our one hour of C.C.D. a week or finish our term on the parish council and get out. We don't need any more grief. Or we may decide to leave the parish altogether. We may even leave the Church. There are many inactive Catholics who followed this route of break in relationship because of a personal disagreement with their pastor.

We can stop everything anywhere along the way. We can turn back and reconcile or we can sever our ties and end our relationship. In that case, we carry the hurt forward into new relationships—always on guard not to be hurt in that way, again. Sometimes the reminder of past pain will cause us to avoid starting a new relationship rather than risk going through that experience again.

When we are in a second marriage, if our new spouse reminds us in any way of the negative behavior of the first, we have an immediate, spontaneous, angry response. If we join a new parish, we carry our own agenda forward with us. We don't move into a quick and easy fellowship; we have our own ideas and our own cause that becomes our benchmark. Instead of reaching out to serve the parish we wait for others to come to us. If we refuse to repent and look at our own faults in these matters, we may also pass our hurts on to others who are innocent bystanders—especially our children.

As we were going through our experiences of trying to integrate our adopted children into our family, it was obvious to us that these were very angry children. They were taking their anger out on us, since we were authority figures and were available to them. One day we said to them, "You know, we think we're paying for sins we never committed." From their case history we know our children were greatly sinned against. Now it was their turn to abuse others.

In a lesser vein, we also realized how we were passing on our own negative behavior to our older children. We were startled one Sunday as we were riding home from church to hear the children laughing at the homily and all the "stupid things" the priest said.

Suddenly we became aware of our own bad habit of criticizing the homilies. It was usually our main topic of conversation after Mass. Unintentionally we had taught our children that they didn't need to respect the priest's opinions or judgments either. They had learned how to criticize by listening to us. We had to change our behavior. It was time to repent.

In order to come to a full acceptance of our need to repent and truly desire change in our lives, we need to pray for the grace of a penitential spirit. This grace helps us get our focus off ourselves and back on others. There are three parts associated with this grace:

1. *Sense of Unworthiness:* A conscious awareness that each of my brothers and sisters in the Body of Christ is filled with the image and likeness of God and the realization of how unworthy I am of their love for me. This is not having a bad self-image, not saying, "How rotten I am." It is about my relative unworthiness because of their great goodness.

2. *Shame for What I Have Done:* A recognition of how I have caused us to be farther apart in our relationship because of what I have done or failed to do.

3. *Gift of Tears:* This is not merely crying, which could be self-pity. Rather, this is a deep cleansing of my spirit by tears of joy as I anticipate our coming back together again.

There are times when one's own prayer for growth in this grace is not sufficient. In addition to asking others to pray for or with us, we find that doing some form of simple penance can be effective. When we ask another person to fast from all solid food or not to smoke or eat between meals until we have achieved a sufficient amount of this grace, we have an increased urgency to overcome our barriers. We have seen some powerful stubbornness overcome in a few hours because one other person was doing a specific penance. As soon as we realize we have achieved the grace we're seeking, we inform our friend so he can stop doing the penance.

When we first began to pray and do penance for growth in grace in this way, it was awkward. We found it hard to believe that God would quickly and bountifully answer our prayers. It seemed to be a contrived, aggressive way of asking for something sacred. At the same time, it seemed to be so simple and straightforward that we did not honestly expect any change in our attitudes or behavior. Having observed it work successfully for ourselves and for hundreds of other people has convinced us that it is an effective way to grow in grace.

We offer one prayer which can be used to ask for growth in the grace of a penitential spirit:

PRAYER FOR A PENITENTIAL SPIRIT

Heavenly Father,
I resist growing in this grace, so it's not easy to request it or to fully open up to it. Help me, Lord, as I pray.
You promised us, Your people, a new heart and a new spirit within us.
Father, I need a new heart. I know I am not fully the person I am called to be by You. Help me to change, Lord. Help me to see where I need to do better.
Father, let me have a sense of my own unworthiness.
Wipe away the false pride,
the air of superiority about me,
the harsh judgments I make about others,
the cynicism and sarcasm that seems to creep out of me.
Let me see the goodness of those You have placed in my life.
Let me see You in everyone I meet.
Give me eyes also to see my own beauty and dignity.
Let me see myself as You see me,
So I can believe more fully
that I too am good and wonderful in Your eyes,
and I have no more need to destroy or humiliate others.

Father in heaven, help me to experience shame for what I have done.
Let me see the real harm and hurt I cause,
hear the rumors and gossip I spread,

see the tears and pain of those I love,
touch the lowered head and know the downcast eyes and slouched shoulders are caused by me.
I believe that if I can see, hear, feel and touch all I have done that has destroyed Your kingdom rather than build it, I will know shame.

Dearest Father, help me also to cry for my sins. Help me let go of my inhibitions and my desire to be in control.
Let my sins be so real to me
that they cause me pain and true sorrow.
Give me the grace I need to sincerely repent.

Father, I don't want to hurt Your people or bring suffering to others, especially those You have sent to be close to me.
Give to me the heart You promised.
Replace this stony heart with a heart of flesh.
Help me to be Your person, bringing You to others.
Let Your love come alive in me
and free me, Lord, from all my illusions.
I ask you this in the name of Jesus.
Amen.

8

Hurting Others

Most of us don't know what we're doing wrong or how we need to change. Very often we're not even aware of how we're hurting others. Sometimes we may even wonder what's wrong with some people when they don't seem to like us or accept us. It's possible that others may be projecting on us their own hostility, but it's also possible that there is a problem within us. When we believe we're always right and the other person is always wrong, we seldom see the need for repentance.

Some of us are also more complacent than others, or less introspective. We don't object to changing, but we honestly can't see where we're doing anything offensive.

In our relationship, we find that Kathy keeps very good track of how John should change to be a better husband and father, and she also doesn't hesitate to tell him about it. John is much less critical and more accepting of Kathy as she is (and of himself too). He almost never complains. It's not that Kathy's perfect; it's just that John is more laid back and relatively less observant of such matters. He also doesn't take offense at most of Kathy's shortcomings.

Whether one chooses to be offended or not however, certain behavior patterns can cause alienation and distrust in family relationships. When we live day by day with someone who is critical, sarcastic or bitter, or have to get along with someone who is indifferent to the state of life in the family, we get worn down. Often a lack of trust develops. A person might think, "If I tell my mother how I feel, will she just use it as an opportunity to cut me down?" Sometimes a wife will lose hope and believe, "He'll never change. He doesn't care about me, and he never will."

To help us sort out where we need to change ourselves, we have put together a checklist of some typical ways we offend one another in families. Many of them are styles of behavior we take for granted and may not see as offensive at all. It's always informative to look at ourselves and ask, "How have I become hard-hearted, Lord? How do I need to change?" As you go through the list, focus on where *you* need to change, not on where your family members should change.

Criticism

Criticism is one of the worst things we can do to one another. Physical abuse destroys the body. Verbal abuse destroys persons—their soul, their spirit, their self-confidence and their self-image. Many good people criticize their loved ones constantly. They call it constructive criticism, but there is no such thing.

> **J**: *For years my relatives have greeted me with the innocent comment, "You're putting on a little weight, aren't you, John?" I was annoyed, especially when it was true, and I already felt bad about my lack of discipline. I took it as an insult and my self-image suffered because of it.*

People who are constantly criticized eventually come to see themselves as worthless. We never feel better about ourselves when we are criticized, and it often causes us to react by refusing to change our behavior even when we know we should.

There is a distinction between correction and criticism. Correction calls for a behavior change, while criticism attacks the person. It's criticism when I say to my teenage son, "You filthy lazy slob; your room is like a pig-pen." In the same situation it is correction when I say, "If your room is not cleaned in thirty minutes you can't use the family car for a week." It's true that we need to correct one another from time to time and we need to teach our children proper behavior. But we have to do it without destroying the person. We can point out a dirty room or bad manners without name calling, screaming, and character assassination. We can address a desired change in behavior without mixing-in insults.

You might like to ask yourself these questions:

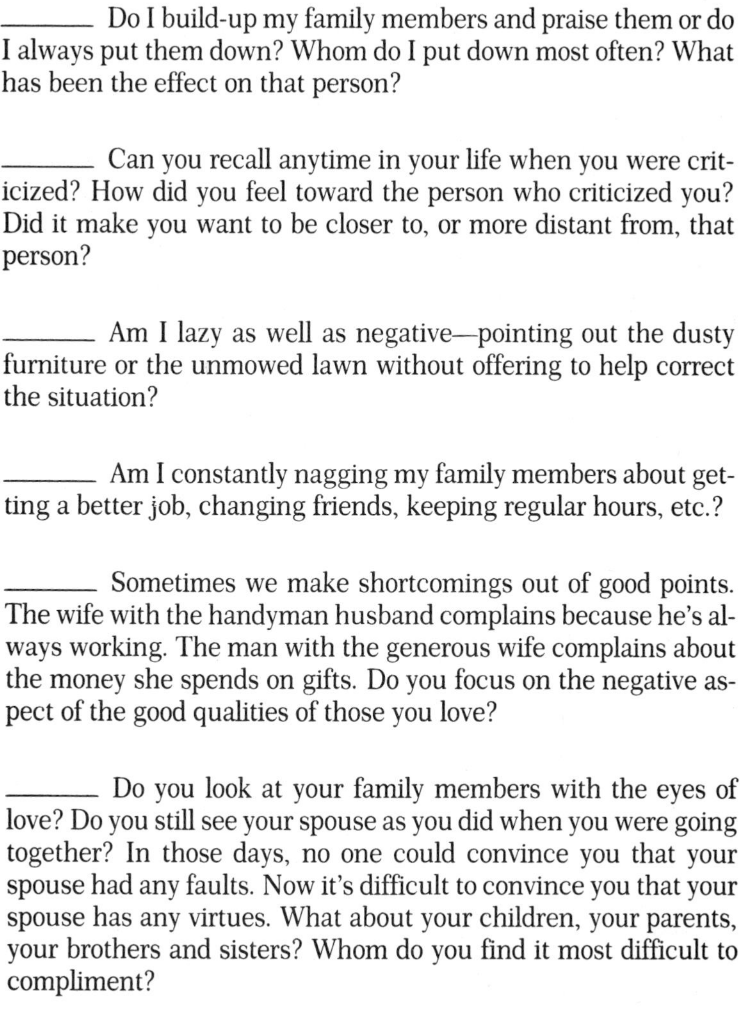

______ Do I build-up my family members and praise them or do I always put them down? Whom do I put down most often? What has been the effect on that person?

______ Can you recall anytime in your life when you were criticized? How did you feel toward the person who criticized you? Did it make you want to be closer to, or more distant from, that person?

______ Am I lazy as well as negative—pointing out the dusty furniture or the unmowed lawn without offering to help correct the situation?

______ Am I constantly nagging my family members about getting a better job, changing friends, keeping regular hours, etc.?

______ Sometimes we make shortcomings out of good points. The wife with the handyman husband complains because he's always working. The man with the generous wife complains about the money she spends on gifts. Do you focus on the negative aspect of the good qualities of those you love?

______ Do you look at your family members with the eyes of love? Do you still see your spouse as you did when you were going together? In those days, no one could convince you that your spouse had any faults. Now it's difficult to convince you that your spouse has any virtues. What about your children, your parents, your brothers and sisters? Whom do you find it most difficult to compliment?

Anger

This does not refer to isolated angry actions. We're considering a pattern of behavior that characterizes our daily behavior. Look at the questions below and see if your behavior pattern fits into any of these descriptions.

_______ Am I a chronically angry person? Do I have moods and certain dispositions when people know that they'd better not bother me? Do I pout and sulk from time to time? Do I withdraw from others and let them know they had better leave me alone? Do I withhold love and affection?

_______ Do I seek to punish others by my behavior? As a wife/husband, do I withhold sex from my spouse? As a son/daughter do I refuse to participate in family activities? As a parent, am I harsh with my children? As a brother/sister do I invite my siblings to come to my house or into my room?

_______ Do I hide behind my busyness? Am I too busy to spend time with my family or with certain members of my family? Do I avoid contact? Do I hug and kiss much less, or not at all? Whom do I hate to touch?

_______ Has anyone ever pointed out my pattern of angry behavior and asked me to change for his or her sake, or to go to counseling?

_______ Do I shout and yell? Am I physically abusive? Do I take out my anger on my family—anger that I bring home from other places and dump on them?

_______ Do I have a hard time accepting any authority?

_______ Am I angry with myself? Do I see myself as missing out on something in life? Am I jealous of others—jealous of the good marriages or the good families they seem to have? Am I jealous of others' good times, good looks, or good income? Do I feel cheated? Do I take it out on myself and my family?

_______ Am I angry with God? Do I believe He has failed me? Do I see my difficulties or disappointments in life (broken marriage, major illness, long term unemployment, poverty, etc.) as at least partly His fault? Does He seem cold and indifferent to me? Do I believe in a loving God or any God at all?

Apathy

The opposite of love is not hate; it is apathy. When we're indifferent to the members of our family, we cut them off. They can't reach us because we won't be touched by them. The walls are up, and we're in hiding.

_______ Married couples can ask: Am I indifferent to my spouse? Do I still burn with passion for him or her? Do I center my day around him or her? Is he or she the first priority in my life—ahead even of our children and our work?

_______ Am I a married person still living as though I were single? Do I still enjoy long afternoons or evenings in front of a TV? Am I a soap opera or sports freak? Do I stay up for the midnight movies and then find it impossible to get out of bed in the morning—or at least impossible to get out of bed in a pleasant mood? Is the amount of time I spend watching TV reasonable, or am I running away from my family?

_______ Am I indifferent to my family? Am I unconcerned about them? Someone may say, "Look, I'll do my thing; you do yours. That way we don't have to bother with each other. I'll be polite and do my share, and keep score to make sure I get my share also." Does that sound like you in any way?

_______ Do I avoid confrontation—getting along as well as possible without being really involved? Do I live like a boarder in my own home?

_______ Do I refuse to socialize with anyone outside our home? Am I becoming a hermit?

Irresponsibility

All of us like to see ourselves as good Christians—responsible people who are doing the best we can. We're not talking about earning a living, although that's a responsibility. We're talking about day-to-day responsibility.

______ Who does the dishes, clears the table, bathes the babies, checks the homework, carries out the garbage? Have we got our chores neatly divided right down the middle—50/50? Jesus asked us to love one another as He loves us—that's 100%? Do we give 100% to each other?

______ Do we share the responsibility for making sure we live within a budget? Who handles the money? Does having my spouse handle the money allow me to be irresponsible? If I am the one who controls the money, do I give my spouse any say in how the money is spent? If I'm in charge of the family budget do I keep a secret slush fund to be used at my discretion?

______ Who makes the decision about whether or not there will be another baby in the family? Is that the woman's problem? Is she blamed if she gets pregnant? Whose babies are they when they arrive? Do they belong to her until they reach a certain age? Who gets up at night with the children? Who takes them to the babysitter? Who handles the discipline?

______ Irresponsibility is an area that teens and single adults living at home need to examine also. Do you see the house as your parents' home and therefore feel that you have no responsibility for maintaining it? Do you resent being asked to help out? Do you see yourself as bestowing a personal favor on the family everytime you participate in family activities?

It is difficult for any of us to admit how offensive our behavior may be to others. Those who are sincerely trying to live a committed Christian life often find it even more difficult to accept that they are hurting others. Yet it is helpful to take time out on a regular basis to listen to what those who love us are trying to tell us by their words and actions. How are we doing? Is our home a better place for everyone because we live there? How can we improve?

Just because our conscience doesn't bother us doesn't always mean that our behavior is wonderful. It could mean we have a weak conscience. Another word to describe our offensive, i.e., hurtful patterns of behavior is "sin." In the First Letter of John we read:

> If we say, "We have fellowship with him," while continuing to walk in darkness, we are liars and do not act in truth. But if we walk in light, as He is in the light, we have fellowship with one another, and the blood of His Son Jesus cleanses us from all sin.
>
> If we say, "We are free from the guilt of sin," we deceive ourselves; the truth is not to be found in us. But if we acknowledge our sins, He who is just can be trusted to forgive our sins and cleanse us from every wrong. If we say, "We have never sinned," we make God a liar and His word finds no place in us. (1 Jn 1:6–10)

Being aware of our own sinfulness is a positive, rather than negative thing. It lessens our self-righteousness and gives us a more balanced view of living in intimate relationships. We have to become aware of the suffering we are imposing on other people so we can begin to search for a way to change our behavior. If you are still unaware of your own negative behavior, stop and think for a minute: What do your family members call you when they are angry with you? There's probably a germ of truth in it, and a clue to how you are hurting them.

9

Why Be Healed?

Our experience is that hurt is never one-sided in a normal, healthy relationship. There is a bi-polarity; a hurt action/reaction. It's as if Newton's laws of motion (for every action, there is a reaction) have their corollary in "laws of relationships." Our spontaneous reaction to being hurt might be benign and neutral, but our considered response afterward is almost always hurtful. Even when we think we're being noble and turning the other cheek, we are in fact usually withdrawn and uninvolved. This may be the best and even the only response possible in a work situation, but when we are living together as a family and one of us is cool and distant, it affects the total atmosphere of the home.

When we are hurt, we see our world through dark glasses; there seems to be little sunshine in our days. We tend to reject others—especially the person who has hurt us. We close off communication and true intimacy. Sometimes we develop an indifference to others—even the innocent victims in our own family. This was certainly true in Sam's case, which is described below.

Sam was in his mid-fifties, married, and the father of five children who were then in the age range sixteen to twenty-five. He was a successful businessman but described himself as a cold and distant father. His wife and children agreed, with the sixteen year old son calling him a "jerk." This situation had troubled Sam all of his married life, and he had sought professional counseling in order to learn how to be the loving, caring father he wanted to be. Nothing seemed to help. He came to one of our Empowerment Workshops.

Shortly after the ceremony of inner healing began he got up and left the room. Assuming he was planning on leaving the

Workshop, Kathy followed him out of the room to ask, "Can I help you in any way?"

Sam replied, "I'm just going outside for a cigarette. After writing about my hurts, I was so deeply touched that I need a breather."

He told Kathy that through prayer and sharing in the Workshop he had come to realize that at the basis of his pattern of offensive behavior with his children was his own hurt which went all the way back to when he had been a little boy. Sam told his story in these words: "When I was growing up, I desperately craved my mother's love and affirmation. But she was a cool, distant person who found it very hard to express her emotions or any affection.

"One warm summer day, when I was about seven years old, I went out into the fields surrounding our house and picked a bunch of wild flowers and brought them to my mother. I really wanted to please her and have her notice me and smile in gratitude. When I gave the flowers to her, she took them from me, and threw them into the garbage. I was devastated. I believe this hurt is causing me to behave in the same distant way with my own children. I need to be free of it so I can love the way I know a father should."

Sam came back in and joined a Small Group to pray for healing. The next morning Sam came into the room with a bright smile on his face a sparkle in his eyes, and a bounce in his steps. Obviously the Holy Spirit had reached into his heart and brought him the gift of inner peace he had so desperately sought for many years. We noticed he brought a small bouquet of roses which he later placed on the altar during the closing Mass.

At the Kiss of Peace, Sam came to Kathy with tears in his eyes, pointed to the flowers on the altar and whispered, "My mother took the flowers." A hurt which had burdened him for over forty years was lifted and he sobbed with joy and thanksgiving. Both Sam and his wife told us later that he was a new man. He was now able to be the warm and loving husband and father he had always wanted to be.

Sometimes our hurts are so alive in us that we get very callous about our behavior with others. We may become cynical or suspicious and be very cautious in our relationships. We might offer conditional love. For example, I may see myself as a thoughtful, caring person. I prove my thoughtfulness by sending cards to my family and friends on all the important holidays and special occasions. I may also buy nice gifts for them. Then it's my day—Mother's Day, my birthday, Valentine's Day—and they forget me, or don't celebrate in a way I deem appropriate. I am furious. "If they really loved me," I think, "they'd do a lot more for me. Look at all I've given them and how little I get back in return."

When a parent doesn't call or write on our birthdays, we might react by deciding not to call him or her either. Consequently, we widen the gap in our relationship rather than reaching out in love in spite of our judgment that the other person was irresponsible. In fact, our own retaliatory behavior is definitely irresponsible. The other person might have been quite innocent; perhaps he or she was ill or simply forgot.

We can become aggressive and demanding of our rights or hyper-sensitive to the intentions of others. In this mode we can't tolerate any type of criticism or correction, even if it's put mildly. We may become cynical.

We found ourselves becoming quite cynical about teenagers at the time when we were having trouble with our younger children. We went to our local shopping mall one evening to find that it was crowded with teenagers hanging out with their friends. We began to observe that they all looked like juvenile delinquents to us. We muttered under our breath about all the local hoods being out. We had never been critical or judgmental about teenagers before and had always enjoyed their company. Now they all looked like the enemy, especially those who were dressed in the latest punk style or in the drug culture fashions.

In this spirit of cynicism, we easily become very defensive and set aside our efforts at building relationships to focus on our rights. We begin to demand those rights and live by the law. Love and trust go out the window. We'll stand on our soap-box and announce with a loud voice:

- "I have the right to a clean kitchen, the right to a neat and tidy house."

- "I have the right to a car that works and my favorite place in the driveway."
- "I have a right to my time in the bathroom."
- "I have a right to a decent night's sleep. From now on, I want everyone home by 10:00 p.m."

When we are acutely aware of selfishness or indifference in those around us, it is often because we have been hurt. Our once easy-going attitude is gone, and law and order prevails.

As a result, we are setting up situations in our lives where others are not free to be themselves. We hold them hostage with our moods and irritability. They have to be continually on guard or risk being on the receiving end of our wrath. They have to agree with us or we'll take it personally. They have to continually prove their love for us—and we're the judge of whether or not they have succeeded in doing that. We don't usually restrict our moody behavior to just the one who hurt us. We keep all our loved ones walking on eggshells. We behave the same way at our workplace, or in school, or with fellow parishioners. We are *not* two different personalities—one type at home and a different type at work.

There is also a ripple effect to hurt. When we hurt, we hurt others, and they in turn pass on their hurts. It's like the cartoon of the man who's hurt by his boss and comes home and shouts at his wife who criticizes their child's behavior. The older child picks on the younger child who kicks the dog who chases the cat . . . who may go back and mess on the man's carpet and start the whole cycle all over again!

In our own lives, we find that when things are going well between us as a couple, they go much better with our children also. We're able to put up with a lot more nonsense or fooling around on their part. However, when we're upset with each other, we're also likely to take it out on the kids, especially on the child who most reminds us of our spouse.

> **K**: *Our son, Johnny, was always very much like his Dad. He was totally charming and could sweet-talk me into just about anything. On days when Johnny would lay on the charm in order to get his way and things were also going well between*

Dad and me, I would smile at him and say, "Ah, Johnny, you're just like your father. You know exactly how to get around me. No, you still can't go to the party, but I give you credit for trying."

On days when I was really angry with John, Johnny got a much harsher response. "Johnny, you're just like your father, and I can't stand it anymore. He thinks he can push me around, and now you're trying it too. Forget it! Go clean your room and leave me alone and don't try that nonsense on me again!" Sometimes I'd deny Johnny permission to do something just because I was in a bad mood, which I blamed on my anger with his father.

We become a hard-hearted people. It's difficult to get concerned about the starving children across the world when we ourselves are starving for affection. It's difficult for us to see the slump in our daughter's shoulders or the hurt look in her eyes when all we can think about is how our own mother criticized us that day for not visiting her often enough.

It's difficult for a mother to feel really enthusiastic about attending a son's ballgame when her heart is aching because of the indifference of his father. We go through the motions with the child, but they are only motions. There is little real joy or pleasure. Or the wife goes to the game just to prove she is superior to her spouse and that aggravates her relationship with him.

When we are hard-hearted we become critical with one another. We look at one another and ask ourselves, "How did I get stuck with you? Whatever happened to the wonderful person I married?" Our children become burdens to us. Gone is the wonder of that little miracle lying in the nursery. Instead we focus on the problem the child now is—the kid who sucks his thumb, wets his bed and throws temper tantrums on Main St. Or we can look at our aging father and forget his kindness to us throughout our lives. Instead we notice how often he repeats himself as he gets older, how boring he is, and how much he tries our patience.

Jesus tells us, "Love one another." We know we should do that, and deep-down we do love. But it's very difficult to act lovingly when we don't feel loving. It's much easier to count the sins of others rather than look too deeply for our own. We know exactly where the other person has failed. So we justify our own behavior. We say things like, "If you had to live with the person I married, you'd behave the same way," or "If you had my mother living with you, you'd know why I am the way I am." The ultimate excuse for justifying our actions is, "I'm only human."

It's precisely at these times, when we most need reconciliation, that we avoid it. "Why should I look at my sins when you're so bad?" We tend not to see our behavior as sinful at all; it's normal under the circumstances. We believe that as long as we don't feel guilty, we're not guilty. We believe that anything we say or do is O.K. At least we're not hurting anyone, but we're not helping anyone either.

We need to be healed, if not for our own sake, then for the sake of others. If we can't see how our own life will be better, then maybe we'll do it so the lives of others will improve. If I can really look at the other people in my life, really see their alienation, their pain, even their fear of me, then maybe I can have some sense of the misery I am causing.

After their first three years with us, our adopted children became more and more hostile. They were openly rejecting us and challenging all our values. It was a very difficult time for all of us. Our self-image as parents was all but destroyed and we were totally exhausted. We turned to God in prayer more and more often and heard—only silence. We watched our reputation deteriorate in the community; some friends turned away from us, and even old friends who offered us their best advice were totally uncomprehending of the depth of our problems.

We removed ourselves from community involvement, and at home we had become rigid disciplinarians. We were trying very hard not to take out our anger or frustration on Brian and Andrea because we didn't want to add to our rift with them, and we knew they were hurting too. So our innocent victims were our older children, whom we ordered to behave or else, and sometimes we victimized one another. We had very little energy left within us, and couldn't tolerate any added dissension.

K: *When I would go to the Sacrament of Reconciliation during this time, I would often speak of my anger and frustration with Brian and Andrea. I would tell how I was taking out these feelings on other family members. I would always go away from the Sacrament with a firm purpose of amendment. I resolved to do better, to change my behavior, to be a kind and loving person in all situations. Within a week, the whole cycle would have begun all over again. I was very frustrated and upset with myself. There had to be a way to break out of that cycle. I didn't know it then, but I needed to be healed.*

Jesus' death on the cross did break this cycle and offer us, through His Body, a means of being healed. We read from Scripture:

> Yet it was our infirmities that he bore, our sufferings that he endured, while we thought him as stricken, as one smitten by God and afflicted. But he was pierced for our offenses, crushed for our sins. Upon him was the chastisement that makes us whole, by his stripes we were healed. (Is 53:4–5)

10

Covering Up the Hurt

When we are hurt we often behave in ways that are not good for us or those we love. Often we don't pay any attention to our own behavior so we're not even aware of it. Or perhaps we're aware of our behavior, but we don't believe it's affecting others. It's like the person who has severely injured his ankle and doesn't get help for it. He's going to "tough it out." There is pain after the initial injury, but he keeps walking on the ankle, waiting for it to heal itself. Eventually, the pain becomes less obvious, so he assumes it's healing. But finding he still must favor the ankle, he walks with a limp. Eventually he may get used to his limp, learn to live with the pain, and imagine himself walking normally. Therefore he considers himself to be cured. But everyone who knows him is aware that he is a man with a limp. He is not healed; he's just "covering up."

Some of us are honestly unaware of ever having been hurt. We have not had any major traumatic or tragic events in life. We believe we have been treated fairly and well—at least as well as could be expected. We mind our own business; we live by the golden rule and so do the others in our lives. Such people sincerely strive each day not only to avoid hurting others, but to help them when they can. This is praiseworthy behavior and to be encouraged.

Yet we read in the First Letter of John: "If we say, 'We have never sinned,' we make him a liar, and his word finds no place in us." (1 Jn 1:10). Sins are offenses directly against God and against the Body of Christ. Consequently in the normal daily events of our lives, each of us is offended by others, and in turn we offend. Therefore each of us has been hurt, even though inadvertently.

We continuously experience hurts throughout our lives, even though we choose not to recognize them as hurts.

Those who find it difficult to identify where they are hurting need to put forth an extra effort to review their lives in order to discover the hurts they have experienced so they can be healed. Where do you "limp"? Where are you most fearful or cautious? Whom do you avoid or gossip about? Particular emphasis should be on actions of omission in relationships. Where is there less warmth, closeness and intimacy in your life than there should be?

Some of us know we've been hurt from time to time in our lives but we have adopted the attitude, "It doesn't affect me." We recall the incidents that happened, but we also recall consciously setting aside our pained reaction quickly. Perhaps we live by the adage, "I don't get mad; I get even." So we live seeking vengeance against those who hurt us. Clearly, anyone who seeks opportunities for revenge is a person whose on-going behavior has been affected by his hurts. Wouldn't it be freeing to be released from the bondage of vengeance?

Another version of such a reaction is the nicer one—the person who "turns the other cheek." If this truly Christian response stops at that and does not involve reasonable attempts at reconciliation, it could actually be a form of superiority. This person thinks, "Even though you are a rotten person, I am going to love you and be nice to you." When we adopt this mode of operation, we can't understand why the other person can't stand us, because we see ourselves as so noble and wonderful.

As young children we often react to hurt by putting up a shield, a pattern of behavior to protect ourselves from experiencing negative feelings. This may appear to work well and certainly helps us get along in circumstances beyond our control, but it also prevents us from forming intimate relationships. As such careful people marry and have families, there may often be a dullness to their lives, a coolness in close relationships, and a real distancing from imposing circumstances that require emotional intimacy. They may substitute sexual activity for emotional intimacy and blandly ask, "Aren't we close? Didn't I make love to you last night?" Or this person may turn off all attempts at intimacy. The word "intimacy" comes from the root words meaning "with fear."

We risk rejection when we decide to trust another person with our private feelings, so instead we don't allow anyone to know us.

Sometimes it helps to be specific in naming the types of behavior patterns which indicate how we act when we have been hurt, and when we are hurting others. We've composed a list of certain behavior patterns that are fairly typical. Go through the list and put a check mark next to any behavior that describes you in the past month. You may check as many as are necessary to describe your behavior. We have alternated using masculine and feminine pronouns to describe the behavior in order to be inclusive. None of this behavior is specific only to men or only to women.

PATTERNS OF BEHAVIOR

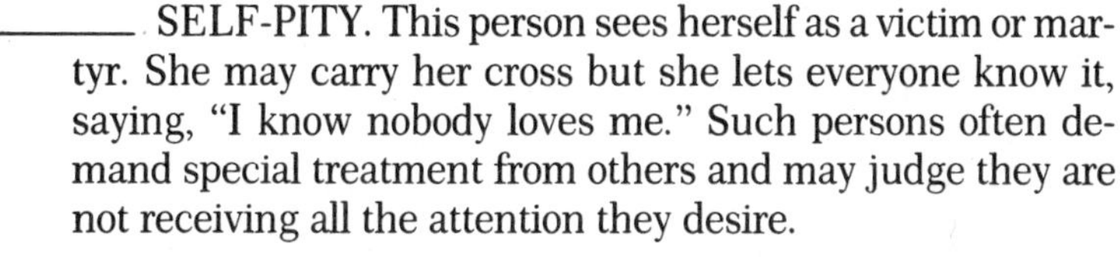

________ SELF-PITY. This person sees herself as a victim or martyr. She may carry her cross but she lets everyone know it, saying, "I know nobody loves me." Such persons often demand special treatment from others and may judge they are not receiving all the attention they desire.

________ SELF-CENTEREDNESS. This person is focused on himself. He has the attitude, "If I can't count on others to make me happy, then I'll make myself happy." He looks out for Number One, failing to see the needs of others around him.

________ INDEPENDENCE. This person says, "I can take care of myself. I have judged you to be less than you should be; therefore I am cutting you out of my life. You can do your thing; I'll do mine. Just don't bother me." This is the attitude which may motivate the young adult who isolates himself from his family or the divorced woman who decides she's been burned in a relationship, and she'll take care of herself.

________ COMPULSIVE SPENDING. When a personal relationship breaks down or fails to satisfy, this person tries to satisfy his need for contentment in owning things. He substitutes things for people, or may try to buy affection, hoping a person will like him because of what he has given to that person.

_______ SCOREKEEPING. This person says, "I am aware of all I have done for you, how good I have been, how hard I have tried. I believe I've done more than my share. I look not at the quality of my own loving, but on what you have given me. What have you done for me lately?"

_______ JEALOUSY. The hurting person is frequently jealous of the happiness of others—especially of the person who has hurt him. He may also be jealous of anyone who seems content, begrudging others a happy marriage, a good home or a wonderful family. There may be a strong streak of self-pity here as well.

_______ DICTATOR. This person may seek power either by manipulating others or by trying to gain control over the lives of others. She assumes the right to define the rules and set all the conditions for a relationship. She is determined to change how others behave, and won't accept any suggestions about how she should change. She might also give God His orders for how He can help.

_______ HARD-HEARTEDNESS. The hard-hearted person can get very stingy with the person who is hurting him. He can be spiteful, spread rumors or gossip, or simply forget a birthday, anniversary or Christmas gift. He may stop speaking or withhold signs of affection. He may be unwilling to spend time playing with the children because he wants to do what he feels like doing, or he may not watch his children participate in sports or school activities because he's too busy.

_______ LACK OF FAITH. This person asks the question, "God, if you are a God, why don't You put a stop to this?" Scripture seems shallow to her, insipid words meant for another time, another place. She may avoid the Sacraments, finding no comfort in the Eucharist and wanting to avoid examining her own conscience in the Sacrament of Reconciliation.

_______ DESPAIR. This person may simply give up on God, believing that God has no interest in him or his problems. To him, life may be more like the crucifixion, without the resurrection. He has no hope.

_______ SELF-RIGHTEOUSNESS. This person is rigid and rule-oriented. She sees herself as right, the other person as wrong. She believes she has been unjustly treated. She may seek out others in order to complain about the one who annoys her. She'll make sure they know her side of the story.

_______ FEAR OF INTIMACY. A hurting person may keep all others at arm's length. He is either unwilling or unable to get close to anyone. He has built walls to protect himself and won't trust anyone ever again.

_______ UNHAPPINESS. An unhappy person finds fault with everything and everyone. Often this person is depressed or tending toward it. She complains endlessly and is often very judgmental and critical of others. She is a "cloudy day person" who seldom notices the sunshine. If she does, she observes, "It won't last long."

_______ ANXIETY. This person is skeptical, cynical, fretting about everything. He always sees the negative side of all situations and expects the worst. He would probably be very concerned about security—saving enough for old age, double locks on the doors, etc. He might worry excessively about his job, about how the kids will turn out, and about almost anything. Life becomes a threatening, fearful challenge for this person, one in which he is defensive and self-centered. He cannot share what he has, because he needs all he has.

_______ COMPULSIVENESS. This person feels compelled to take immediate action to solve every problem. She'll often react with only partial information. She is the one who will say, "Don't just stand there; *do* something." She might also tend to eat or drink too much. She may fear boredom so she always has a full schedule of activities. When she senses the first signs of illness, she looks for a magic pill which will instantly remove all discomfort and suffering. A compulsive person might work extreme hours even though it causes her inordinate stress each day.

_______ MALICIOUSNESS. This person seeks revenge against others and is envious of what they have. He might even wish them to suffer sickness, pain or loss. This type of person plays "dirty tricks" on others and thinks it's cute or funny. He may gossip about someone's behavior or purposely withhold compliments because he knows it will hurt another. He may stop talking to certain family members in order to punish them for something.

_______ ABANDONMENT. This person generally assumes that God's grace won't work to change a situation or another person. It is denying the truth of scripture, for Jesus said, "With God everything is possible." It is giving in to the nagging doubts that perhaps God has forgotten him in the midst of his suffering. It is the parent who decides a child is a lost cause and so gives up on him. In a spirit of abandonment, a woman may give up on her marriage. She hasn't divorced, but she has become totally involved outside the house. At home, she is too busy to get too close with anybody. Many husbands do the same. This could also be the child who gives up on his parents or brothers and sisters and avoids contact with the family.

_______ HARSHNESS. This person ignores the little things of life that make living together more joyful. He doesn't open the car door for his wife, is quick to make a sarcastic comment, is abrupt in conversations, and is critical of how much is spent on gifts. He assumes other people deliberately set out to upset him by coming home late, or spilling the milk, or forgetting to mow the lawn, or failing to clean up the dinner table, etc. He is not affectionate or affirming. He displays a general insensitivity to concerns of others in the family.

______ AGGRESSIVENESS. This person is pushy or assertive in pursuing her own interests. In the area of sexuality, she is insensitive to her spouse's needs. On the dating scene, she may deny another's choice of chastity and push for sexual activity. This is also the person who indulges in pornography. As an aggressive person, she might also be physically or psychologically abusive of herself or others. She may constantly put other people down or set out to destroy someone's self-image. She may call another stupid or uneducated and criticize his opinions. She may isolate a person from blood family members so she can control him.

______ INTRIGUED WITH EVIL. This person spends a great deal of time and effort learning about evil. He focuses on the worst articles in the daily paper or on the TV news, and wants to know all about the latest gossip, scandal, or horror story. He relishes bad news or grisly news items and spend much time and energy going over the details. He gradually loses his innocence and becomes filled with distrust and cynicism. Jesus' message to love one another has no room in his heart.

______ SEVERITY. This person over-reacts to situations. When her twelve year old son doesn't clean his room, she punishes him by grounding him for two months. When her husband comes home late for dinner, she refuses to talk to him for a week. She consistently takes extreme positions or actions when much more lenient options might be chosen.

As you go through the list and think about your own behavior, you probably do see how you have been hurt or how you are hurting others in your family, at least some of the time. Most likely, you have also identified the behavior of someone you love who has hurt you. Our reasoning then usually is, "How can I get *them* to change? Then I won't be the victim of their behavior anymore."

Obviously the best thing for everyone would be for their beloved to be healed. If they'll go, try to persuade them to attend a healing service, or pray for healing with them yourself. However, not all people are ready or willing to have healing take place. Then we have to back off and work on our own healing. Such persons may, or may not, come around eventually, but in the meantime, as healed persons, we will be able to love them just the way they are.

When you are looking at your own hurts, don't worry about whether you think they are too big or too insignificant. Not all the hurts in life are big $5,000 hurts. Most are much less—more like twenty-five cent hurts. A hurt is still a hurt, and when we hurt, we do not have inner peace nor do we bring inner peace.

We believe that in order to protect ourselves from further hurt, we adopt certain of these behaviors and wear them most of the time. We make them part of our identity. It's how we see ourselves and how others see us. Soon we forget how we ever were different. The only problem with wearing this identity is that it's false. It is not who we are or who we are called to be. Thomas Merton wrote that someday when we arrive in heaven and present ourselves to the Father with this false image, God will ask us, "Who are you? I know you not."

Jesus has said, "Trust me when I tell you that whoever does not accept the kingdom of God as a child will not enter into it." (Lk 18:17) It's hard to have the love, the trust, the joy and the simplicity of a little child when we are hurt.

11

Learning How To Forgive

A major key to inner peace is inner healing. We cannot have peace when we are not ourselves. We cannot be ourselves when we are hurt. Somehow we have to come to the point where we can let go of the hurts in our own lives and the lives of our family members and put them in God's hands. This sounds easy. Many times we thought we had done it, but we never really let go. Later we realized that we had to first forgive whoever has hurt us in order to be free ourselves. We cannot be healed as long as we're harboring bitterness in our hearts.

What is forgiveness? First consider some limited concepts we often use for forgiveness. Forgiveness is *not* just calming down and not being angry. It is *not* just giving up our desire for retaliation. It is *not* just letting go of our grudges. Forgiveness contains all those qualities, but it is so much more. Forgiveness is truly setting aside everything in order to focus on the beloved.

When we forgive, we discover ourselves. We learn that our identity is to be both lover and beloved. Because we've been hurt, we haven't been great lovers nor have we allowed ourselves to be beloved. When we offer forgiveness, it has to come not from our superiority, as perfect Christians, but from a true sense of humility and compassion. We have to have a profound inner awareness of the goodness of whoever has hurt us . . . to recognize the image and likeness of God that is in them.

We have to be willing to give up our case and our cause—even if we think we were right, and we are certain every jury in the country would agree with us. We have to listen to Jesus when He says, "Remove the plank from your own eye first; then you will see clearly to take the speck from your brother's eye." (Mt 7:5b) We have to be willing to take a big risk.

We believe true forgiveness is more than an act of the will. Often we say we've forgiven when what we mean is that we've given up, or dropped the issue. One way to see where we are in forgiving is to put it on a scale of One to Ten where One means, "I really haven't forgiven at all," a Five means, "I'm about halfway there," and a Ten means, "I've totally, all-out forgiven the person, and I see his or her wonder and beauty." Then I can love the other person, at least from a distance. This type of deep inner forgiveness is a grace from God. It comes through our own prayer and desire for it and also through the intercessory prayer of others.

Sometimes the hurt we have experienced is so intense that we find it nearly impossible to forgive the one who hurt us. An example of this is Michael, a man we met on an Empowerment Workshop. Michael had described his hurt by saying that six years before, his son was killed by a hit-and-run driver. Michael said that he was so angry with the unknown driver that he would kill him if he ever found him.

This anger had spilled over into every aspect of Michael's life. He had begun physically abusing his wife. He refused to be close to his two children, born since the accident, because he feared losing them also. He was depressed, and for two years had been unemployed and uninterested in searching for a job. Night and day he was plagued by his obsession to find the person who killed his son so he could, in turn, kill him. His pain was so deep that he could not bring himself to forgive this unknown person, the killer of his little boy. When his group began praying for Michael to grow in the grace of forgiveness, he was stalled at a minus Two on the scale of plus One to Ten!

As the group prayed over him, Michael was able to move to a plus Two. Then they paused to discuss for a few minutes any barriers Michael might have to forgiving the man who killed his son. He spoke of his frustration, his hurt, his indignation, his fear of the future. One by one, the group prayed that each of these obstacles would be lifted. As they were gradually overcome, forgiveness began to grow in Michael's heart. Finally the group asked Michael to describe his son to them.

Michael spoke of a little boy who was the fulfillment of his dreams, a child who blended the qualities of both his mother and father and reflected their love. They asked him, "Would your little son in heaven want to see his father so burdened and held captive by his anger?"

Michael replied, "I know he wouldn't want that."

The group asked, "Would you be willing to place your pain, your anger, your hurts in the hands of your son and let him take them to Jesus to be healed?"

Michael answered, "Yes."

As Michael let go, the group could see the tightness and hostility in his face dissolve. Joy transfigured him. They could tell just by looking at him that he was healed. Together they rejoiced, and Michael shared the story of his healing with the whole group.

A year later, Michael was still the same gentle, kind and loving husband and father he had been before his son's death. He had gotten a new job at which he was doing well. Filled with inner peace, Michael was able to begin again and deal with all the factors of his life.

Like Michael, most of us have barriers that prevent us from letting go of our hurts. Here are a few:

Self-righteousness:

"The other person has hurt me and is more guilty than I am." But who is to determine that? Who is capable of saying who is the greater sinner or who inflicted the greatest pain? Just by asking the question, we show we have not accepted the virtues of compassion and humility.

Fear of being hurt again:

We don't trust the other person—especially if we know we have to go home and face him. We don't ever want to risk loving like that again because we don't want to repeat that hurt. We believe that at least with our anger, our defenses are active, and our enemy is less likely to be able to get to us. But if we live as hurting people, we are still suffering. It's better to take the risk, step out in trust, and be fully alive in God, than half-dead in our own apathy or indignation.

Fear of being misunderstood by others:

Sometimes we are afraid to give up a hurt because we think our forgiveness will be misunderstood. Others may think we approve of what happened, or we don't really care about it. It's possible that other people might think that of us, but that's beside the point. Forgiveness has nothing to do with approval. It has everything to do with filling us with the light of Christ.

Fear of communicating with the person who hurt me:

"I can't go to the person who hurt me and tell her I forgive her." We are not suggesting that we have to do that. First, it's not always possible. Sometimes the person we need to forgive has died or has moved away. Sometimes the person is old or sick and isn't even aware she has hurt us. We don't need to lay a guilt trip on that person at this point in their lives. At other times, the person may be totally indifferent to the fact that she has hurt us. She just doesn't care. Going back to a person like this to tell her you have forgiven her only invites further hurt.

We are asking simply that you forgive her *in your heart*. After you have forgiven and been healed, you can always decide what action, if any, should be taken. The difference is that now any action you decide upon will be chosen as a healed person rather than as a hurting person. If it's someone in your household and you decide that you can't live with that person again, at least it will be a decision made with deep regret, not out of hatred or a desire for revenge.

Self-Pity:

Sometimes we enjoy being a martyr. It may even have become part of our identity. Everyone in the parish feels sorry for us because of our terrible husband/child/or mother. We like having people know how we suffer. Maybe if we're healed we'll become aware of how we've been causing hurt to others, and we'll have to change our behavior, and reach out to them.

Rationalizing:

As good, loving people we most often tend to rationalize our hurts. We claim we don't need to forgive anyone because no one has ever really hurt us, at least not intentionally. We say our mother neglected us because of her own deprived childhood. Our spouse abuses us because he can't help himself. Our friend left us because we're not very good company. Our child refuses to go to church because she didn't receive adequate training. Yet those who know us know our pain is real and negatively affects how we live our daily lives. We have an obligation to the Body of Christ to get healed; it is irrelevant why someone hurt us. We have to take responsibility for our own lives.

But I'm right . . . :

It doesn't matter if we are right or wrong, we have to forgive. This is what Jesus meant when He told us, "Love your enemies." Jesus' advice is tough.

We need to stop worrying about what others will think of us. We have to go all out, put ourselves in God's hands and pray for the grace of forgiveness.

Sometimes it helps to clarify whom we should forgive. We find three general categories.

1. *Another person.* Sometimes it's very obvious who has hurt us. We recall the incident or series of incidents that offended us. Sometimes it's a little more obscure. It could be a whole group of people who hurt us or even a corporation. Then we would suggest focusing on only one or two people if possible. Who were those most responsible? Who had the most authority or power in the group? Who were the ringleaders?

2. *Ourselves*. The person we expect the most from is usually ourselves. When we fail, we can be very hard on ourselves. Maybe we have made bad decisions or good decisions that turned out badly. Maybe we have failed to love enough. Maybe we have regrets over our past: the education we didn't get, the children we didn't bother with, the parent we didn't visit often enough. Maybe we believe we have failed ourselves, maybe we have failed others. The question is: Can you forgive yourself for at least one specific incident that you still haven't let go?
3. *God*. When our granddaughter died, Kathy was very angry with God. Frequently when we have suffered for no apparent reason, we blame God. This would include death of a loved one, miscarriage, chronic pain or sickness, accidents, handicaps, damage from natural events like fire, tornados, floods, etc. Sometimes we also blame God when our lives don't turn out as we had planned. Kathy wanted to have a large family of ten children. When we were only able to give birth to three, she blamed God and herself. She thought God didn't like her very much or didn't think she was a good mother.

Sometimes it's not immediately obvious whom we need to forgive, and we have to work at it for a while to sort it out. For example, a woman might be laid off from her job and blame the management of the company. Later she may be angry with God for the difficult circumstances that she's in, the fact she must work to support her family, etc. Finally, after a great deal of soul-searching, she may find that she needs to forgive herself. Deep inside she may be angry with herself for not having acquired the skills she needs, or for deciding to work for a particular company, or for a variety of personal decisions she made in the past which have led her to this situation. It's helpful to continue searching for underlying causes of hurt when an initial attempt at seeking healing doesn't seem to achieve everything desired.

It's also important to remember that while some healing occurs very quickly, it may take time to heal other hurts. Our experience is that often even very deep hurts are healed swiftly when a person is ready to let go of them—usually because one no longer wants to be burdened in that way. Other hurts, even relatively simple ones, appear to hang on for some time. Healing cannot be forced, so continue to place the hurt in God's hands, pray and ask for prayer. Sometimes professional counseling may also help.

After Brian ran away and Andrea chose to live in an institution rather than return home, we were devastated. Our instinctive response to the whole situation was to write them off and say, "So long." Yet, we had made a commitment to these children when we adopted them. We promised we would be their parents forever. The only problem was that they didn't want us—at least at that time.

We had another question that kept eating at us also. How could they come to believe in God's love for them if they didn't experience human love? How could they believe in a loving Father in heaven who would always care for them if they never experienced a loving father on earth? Would the word "Father" always have a bad ring to it? We wanted to love our children.

We prayed for the grace to forgive them. We focused on one child at a time. We focused on only one incident at a time. Could we forgive Brian for running away? Then, could we forgive Brian for breaking into our house? With Andrea it was similar. Could we forgive Andrea for telling stories about us? Could we forgive her for rejecting us? Little by little we worked our way through. First, we wrote down briefly the incident that caused the hurt. Second, we wrote down our feelings, then and now. Third, we wrote how we were hurting others because we were hurt. Finally, we wrote of our desire to forgive and any barriers we thought we had to forgiving.

The writing helped us get it all out. Writing helps us get below the surface and reveal deeper attitudes, opinions, and feelings than simply talking about them. It helps get us out of an argumentative, problem-solving mode and into a calmer, listening mode. It helps us focus more on the others in our lives and be less concerned with our own self-pity and self-righteousness.

The sharing we did with one another after that helped us experience the love and understanding of at least one other person. Then we prayed for the grace of forgiveness. If John was praying with Kathy, he would lay hands on her and ask God to pour the grace into her. He would ask God to lift any barriers or fears she had to forgiving. After a period of prayer, he would ask if there had been any movement within Kathy to forgive. On a scale of 1–10, where was she? If there was no movement, we looked for more barriers, and prayed some more.

Having a strong desire to be healed and a realization that we were not ourselves when we're hurting caused us to really want to let go of all the pain and disappointment we were experiencing. We really worked at it, and we were healed. We have included a copy (at the end of this chapter) of what we did if you wish to use it with a spouse, trusted friend or a small circle of confidants.

We believe God wants us to be healed. He wants us to be His Alleluia people and reflect His peace, His love, His joy. After we were healed, we were able to begin again in our relationship with Brian and Andrea. We knew where Brian was living, so we contacted him there and let him know we were thinking of him. At Christmas time, we bought him gifts as though he was still at home. The older children delivered the gifts, and Brian even came for a short visit. He let us take him out to lunch on his birthday a few months later.

We visited Andrea at her new school. We wrote to her and spoke of our love for her. Since gifts were important to her as a sign of love, we would usually bring her something when we visited. For a long time, she no longer called us Mom and Dad, but Mr. and Mrs. For a long time there was a lot of anger, but gradually that lessened.

Our spiritual director helped us understand how we needed to adjust our parenting of Brian and Andrea at this time in our lives. She suggested this metaphor to us, "Imagine an outstretched hand with fingers spread apart. Neither push your children away from you, nor pull them toward you. Let your children choose to come or go." We also had to allow them to slip through our fingers if they wished. She helped us understand that we were responsible *to* them, not responsible *for* them.

As healed persons, we found that we were making decisions differently than we had before. We no longer had any desire for revenge or retribution. On the other hand, we no longer felt guilty about any shortcomings we had. As healed people we would decide what we could do and would do, and then we did it. If the children asked for special help, we'd also decide whether or not we could respond to the request. If we could, we did. If not, we offered whatever we could. In other words, we began to treat them like our other children, with whom we had a very good relationship.

God had really blessed us. Our initial healing in our relationship with Brian and Andrea took place on an Empowerment Weekend experience. When we came home we called our older children to let them know what had happened to us. They all commented that we even sounded different than we had before. Even over the telephone, they sensed our inner peace.

We found that we were also deeply joyful. Just as our capacity for pain had increased with all the rejection we had experienced, so had our capacity for joy. It was as though a well had been dug deeper in us. As our healing progressed, our enthusiasm for life and creative work returned more strongly than ever. We were well blessed, but there was still more to come.

A PRAYER PROCESS FOR INNER HEALING

Here is a brief description of a healing prayer process that can be used whenever needed. The person who is hurting asks a trusted, close friend to pray with him. This might be a husband and wife, a parent and child, or any two friends. Meet in a quiet place in your home at a time you won't be disturbed for a while. Then go through the following steps:

1. The hurting person writes a description of his hurt. Include a brief description (one paragraph) of the actual incident when the hurt occurred. Also describe briefly (one paragraph) how you felt then.
2. Next write in some detail how you feel *right now*. Try to get below the surface feeling and down to your strongest feeling. In other words, even though this hurt may have originally occurred some time ago, it still hurts today when you think about it. It is today's pain for which you are seeking healing.

3. This hurt affects your behavior today, particularly with those who are closest to you. How are you hurting them? Be specific. Give their names and say how you're treating them.
4. Then write where you are on forgiving the person who hurt you. (Try to use the scale of 1 to 10 to indicate this.) What barriers do you have to forgiving this person who hurt you? What do you fear will happen to you if you forgive him/her?
5. Then write how you're going to change your behavior as a result of being healed. Who will benefit most from your healing? How will they benefit?
6. Spend as long as you need writing—at least fifteen minutes.
7. When your writing is done, read your response to your prayer partner (directly from the page).
8. The other person listens intently, trying to take on the reader's feelings. Then the listener describes back to the reader those feelings, using his or her own experiences of these same feelings. This dialogue goes on between the two until the reader says he is satisfied that the listener has sincerely understood the feelings he described.
9. Then the listener asks the reader, "Can you forgive the person who hurt you?"
10. The reader answers by stating how much of the grace of forgiveness he has right now, using a scale of 1 to 10 where 10 is maximum, to state where he is.
11. Then both pray together until the reader achieves a sufficient amount of this grace of forgiveness. Use any form of prayer you wish (the traditional prayer of the Church, praying in tongues, reading Scripture, spontaneous prayer, etc.). Periodically the listener asks the reader where he is now with the grace. When the listener says he has reached at least an 8 out of 10, that is an indication he is ready to forgive the one who hurt him, and thus to accept healing. (This step is essential to the healing process. It may be necessary to take the person, step by step, through any barriers he has until they are all lifted. You may also ask them if they'll give up their hurt for the sake of the persons who would benefit from their healing.)

12. Then the listener places his or her hands on the reader's head and says, "In the name of the Body of Christ, be healed." Spend some time in prayer of thanksgiving.
13. Then tell others of all God has done for you, so they too will know He is at work in the lives of His people.

We find that praying with a crucifix enriches our experience. Select a crucifix which has personal meaning in your life (wedding gift, belonged to my grandmother, was in my father's casket at his funeral, was a first Holy Communion gift, etc.) and tell your prayer partner(s) about its meaning to you. Then hold the crucifix while you read aloud about your hurts and while you are going through the healing dialogue and prayer. As a final step in the process, place your hurts on the body of Christ on the cross and ask Him to absorb them in His infinite suffering.

Be patient with yourself and the person you are praying with. If healing doesn't occur immediately, God has not abandoned you. He loves you intensely. It may be necessary to go through a healing prayer process that extends over a longer period of time or to try another type of healing such as a healing prayer service at church.

12

Love Your Enemies

> Two others who were criminals were led along with him to be crucified. When they came to Skull Place, as it was called, they crucified him there and the criminals as well, one on his right and the other on his left. Jesus said, "Father, forgive them; they do not know what they are doing." They divided his garments, rolling dice for them." (Lk 23:32–34)

We always thought this was a nice model for how we should behave. We were to forgive, no matter how difficult the case, no matter how right our cause. It's a good idea, but is it possible? For a long time we believed it was not. We believed that it was easy for Jesus to say this. After all, He was God—a man of perfect virtue. We were only human and very imperfect.

Then one Monday in early September 1982, we received a phone call telling us that our son had been murdered. He was camping in the Rocky Mountains with his friends. A young woman and her boyfriend were camping nearby. That morning the young woman had awakened—"feeling irritable," she said. She took her rifle and started shooting at various targets. Eventually she spotted Johnny, washing out the silverware from breakfast at the water spigot.

"Watch me scare that fella."

She aimed her rifle, pulled the trigger, and put a bullet into his heart. He was dead almost immediately. They had never met, never spoken. There was no reason. He was an innocent victim. It was 10:30 a.m. in a campground filled with families.

We were both on the phone when Tom, Johnny's roommate, called with the news. Our hands started shaking, our eyes clouded with tears, and we could barely talk. "Are you sure,

Tom?" we kept asking him. "Are you really sure? Is he dead or only injured?"

"He's dead, Mr. and Mrs. Colligan. He's really dead. I was there. I saw it happen."

How can this be? Three days earlier we had talked to him. He was alive, looking forward to his camping trip. We told him to be careful and have a good time. We had bought his camping equipment ourselves. He loved to camp; we all did. We had camped since the children were little. It was good to live outside with nature—it was safe.

We put the phones down, went into our bedroom and held each other for several minutes. Then we reached for the crucifix hanging over our bed, our wedding crucifix, and began to pray.

"Dear Jesus, we don't understand what is happening in our lives or what this is all about. We thought we had been through the worst that could happen. We never dreamed of anything like this. Heavenly Father, we are walking in a mystery that gets deeper and darker all the time. We don't know where we are going, but we trust that somehow You are there in all of this. Somehow You have Your arms around us even though we don't see You or feel You.

"Be with us, Father, as we go through these next few days and weeks to come. Be with us as we prepare our children, mothers and family for the death of our son. Bring us together, Lord. Help us to be one with You."

The Wednesday after Johnny was killed, his body was flown in from Denver. The plane was arriving after 11:00 p.m., so the undertaker suggested we not go out to meet it. He promised to be there for us.

K.: *We went to bed early that night, around 10:00 p.m., but I couldn't sleep. I kept saying the Jesus Prayer over and over again, "Lord Jesus Christ, Son of the living God, have mercy on me, a sinner. Lord Jesus Christ . . . " Suddenly there was a round ball of bright light in the room. It stood there for a few minutes and I knew immediately that it was Johnny.*

I was filled with joy at his presence. The light came forward and settled on the bed between John and me. It seemed perfectly content to be there, as though it belonged there. There was an incredible sense of peace about it—a deep, profound peace, unlike anything I had experienced. I knew then that Johnny was in heaven for sure. He was with our Father. He was O.K. I relaxed and basked in his presence.

After a while, the light began to move. It went into a smaller and smaller ball, and came into my heart. Johnny was home for good! I looked at our bedside clock. It was shortly after 11:00 p.m. Welcome home, Johnny!]

The funeral was the following Friday. The family came and then returned to schools or homes. Our friends departed. There was silence. The leaves began to fall from the trees as we moved into the rain and frost of October. Still, the sun shone through the now bare branches and the apparent deadness and emptiness around us. We began to take long walks; we needed to be outside. Sometimes we talked; sometimes we were quiet, absorbing the atmosphere.

There must be an answer. There are seasons in nature, seasons in life. What does it mean? Even as we knew that the trees and flowers weren't really dead, we also were certain that Johnny lived; he was with us in spirit.

Still, in the months that followed there was a tremendous loneliness. We got busy with our work. John became a workaholic—starting at dawn and working until almost bedtime. Kathy couldn't seem to settle on anything—fussing here and there but not accomplishing much.

We went on another Empowerment Weekend, presented by Fr. Chuck Gallagher. This time when we were asked to write about our greatest hurt, we each wrote about our son's death. Each of us went to pray with separate groups of people. Both of our groups told us they couldn't heal us of our grief. It was too fresh, too strong. Besides, it was a natural process that took time—perhaps a lifetime. They were very wise people. Both groups read more into what we had written. What they saw in John was a man who was out of control in his life. His adopted children rejected him, his daughters were away from home, his son was dead, and he had just switched jobs. Everything that he had worked for and valued most was swept away. He had latched onto his work as a refuge—something he could control. Could he give up his fear of losing control? Would he like to be healed of that? He would.

For Kathy, there was a deep sense of despair. She had no hope for the future. Christmas was coming, but she had no plans, no desire for Christmas. She was ignoring it, hoping it wouldn't come. "Why plan?" she thought. "Who knows who will come home? Maybe nobody will come. Maybe we'll all be dead anyway."

Would Kathy like to be healed of her hopelessness, her fear of the future? She would. They prayed over us and asked God to send us the graces of courage, hope, and trust in Him. He did, and we were healed. We celebrated Christmas in a quiet but peaceful way. We settled into a normal daily routine of work, exercise, recreation, and prayer. We were also able to comfort the children as they arrived for the holidays. Everyone came home for Christmas.

The days began to get brighter; spring was approaching. The young woman who shot Johnny was coming to trial in Colorado. We were not going out for it, but the district attorney asked us to send a letter, addressed to the court, describing Johnny: What was he like? What kind of person was he? What did he mean to the family? How did his death affect us?

It took us a week to write the letter. As we reflected back on our son's life, we realized what a gentle person he was. He used to march with us to protest the war in Vietnam. He put his toy guns away after Martin Luther King was killed. He wanted to be either a priest, a social worker, or a probation officer. He staffed the school retreats and witnessed to his relationship with God. When he registered to vote, he registered in the Right to Life Party. He registered for the draft but only to keep his mother happy.

We asked ourselves, "What would Johnny say if he could be in court for this trial?" We knew without a doubt that he would forgive the person who shot him. He was like that. He forgave everybody all the time—even when we sometimes thought he was being a sucker. Johnny could never dislike anyone.

We wrote this in our letter to the court. We told them we

knew our son forgave his killer. We asked them to be sure to tell her that. We knew that we too needed to forgive. We hadn't even begun to deal with this, but now we were ready. We brought out our crucifix and prayed together once again. We poured out on the cross all our hurt, anger, bitterness, frustration, and sorrow. We asked Jesus to absorb it and carry it for us.

Then we prayed for the grace of forgiveness, asking God to lift all our doubts and fears about it. He did. We were healed. We felt deeply peaceful. We wrote in our letter that we forgave also. "Please tell her that for us. Make sure she understands."

We don't see ourselves as soft on crime. Some people deserve to be punished. Some are very dangerous. Some should probably be imprisoned for life. Probably most have some psychiatric problems that should be addressed. But we feel strongly that death is not ours to bring to another. Having lost a child to death, we would not wish to have anyone else also lose a child, even if that person was a murderer. More than that, we don't believe we can be believable witnesses to the good news of Jesus Christ if we are filled with a desire for revenge. That is not what He taught us. He was a man of peace.

As we went through Holy Week that spring, we meditated on the passion. Having lost a son, we had a keen appreciation for what Mary was going through. How much more cruel it must have been for her because she was also a witness to His slow, deliberate death. As we drew near Good Friday and those words, "Father, forgive them; they do not know what they are doing," we thought of Mary at the foot of the cross. We realized that she too must have forgiven; otherwise she would have become a very bitter, angry person. There is no way she could have been the woman of peace that she was.

The apostles and holy women must have also forgiven, or they could never have lived among Jesus' killers. They could never have returned to teach. They would never have been credible witnesses to the healing power of God. They must also have forgiven themselves for their own failures and shortcomings. They all forgave—everyone except Judas, who could not.

We pray with one another every day. When we are praying for healing, we always pray together, and sometimes with one or two other people. We like to spend a few minutes first, talking out or preferably writing out all the feelings and frustrations within. Then we lay hands on the person seeking healing and pray for the grace of forgiveness as well as a lifting of any barriers. We have included a prayer for forgiveness that you can use alone or with a group if you would like. Just put yourself in God's hands, trust Him, and be at peace.

A FORGIVENESS PRAYER

Dear Father,

We invite You to be here with us today. Come and sit among us, talk to us, touch us with Your love. Do more than that—wrap Your arms around us and let us feel Your presence here with us.

Father, light up the corners of our hearts so we can see where You want to heal us today.

Do you want me to forgive *myself*?

> Father, I forgive myself for all the times I have failed. For the times when I failed myself—when I could have done something and I didn't—when I shouldn't have said something and I did—for the bad decisions I have made—for failing to live up to my own high expectations for myself.
>
> Father, I forgive myself for all the times I have failed others—for the times I wasn't there for them, when I couldn't listen or didn't care—for the times I was too tired or too self-centered or too busy—or just plain not interested.
>
> Father, show me the love You have for me. Help me to accept and enjoy my own humanity. Help me to appreciate that I am not the Messiah—You are. Help me to love being me—just the way You made me.

Do You want me to forgive *another person*?

> Father, I forgive my family of origin for all they have done or failed to do for me —For the times when they didn't love me, or love me as I needed to be loved—for the affection I didn't receive—for the attention I craved and they never no-

ticed—for the times when they abandoned me or left me with others—for all the needs in me I was never able to express and they were never able to see, Father, I forgive them.

Father, I forgive my own family members: my spouse who has offended me, failed to listen to me, ignored me, puts pressure on me to be someone I'm not; my children who make great demands of me, who take me for granted, who don't appreciate me or see me as a real person.

Father I forgive those others in my life whom I believe have not been faithful to me. For those who have gossiped about me, put me down, ignored me, or were downright offensive to me. I forgive those who have caused injury or harm to my family—those who have victimized us in any way. I give them all back to You, Lord. I don't want to be a judge anymore. I want to be free and trusting.

Father, do You want me to forgive *You*?

Sometimes I blame you, Father, for the way things are. I don't understand why the world is the way it is. I don't know why people suffer, why babies die, why good people know poverty, pain, starvation.

Father, I can accept it when the wicked are punished, but often the evil ones seem to go free—and that bothers me.

Father, it especially bothers me to see those I love suffer. I can take it for myself, but I don't want bad things to happen to my parents, my brothers and sisters, and most especially my children, nieces or nephews. Father, these are the little ones you have given me to care for—and in their pain, I experience my own helplessness. That's when I get angry.

Father, I hate to see nature violated. When animals suffer, I suffer too. When living things are destroyed by carelessness or stupidity, I die a little bit myself.

Father, I give to You today . .
my anger
my self-pity
my indignation

my self-righteousness
I give You my fears . . .
of having to change my behavior
of worrying how other people will interpret my behavior
of being hurt again.

Father, I give You my whole life today as I have lived it thus far. You carry it for me on Your cross.
Today I begin anew—today is a resurrection day.
Today I am free to be me.

Amen.

13

Our Lady of Peace

Our search for peace would not be complete without Mary. As Catholics, we come from a tradition in our Church of love and devotion to our Blessed Mother and the saints. Both of us were raised with that tradition—May altars, crowning of the Blessed Mother, hymns to Mary, wearing Miraculous Medals, reciting the daily rosary as a family in May and sometimes in October as well. When our children were born, we dedicated them to Mary at the time of their Baptism because we wanted Mary to watch over each of them.

Still, Mary was a mystery to us. Who was this silent woman? As we went through the 1960's and early 1970's she seemed less real and less relevant all the time. We no longer said the rosary, prayed special novenas to her or wore our medals. We didn't teach our children about Mary either. We put her statue away in the bedroom.

The books we read about her at this time seemed to portray a woman who was too sweet and too pious. How could men and women of our time relate to someone so perfect?

> **K**: *One day while I was praying, Mary came to mind. I asked God to help John and me to get to know His mother better—to begin to see her as a real person like ourselves. Soon she became a companion. I would be washing clothes, cooking a meal, or sweeping the floor and suddenly think: Mary must have done this too. I'd be talking to one of the children and think about how she must have talked to Jesus—even gotten angry with Him.*

When we decided it was time for us to become adoptive parents, St. Joseph was the only foster parent we knew. We asked Joseph and Mary to be with us. We dedicated Brian and Andrea to them. We brought out our statue of Mary and placed her in the living room. We created a small shrine to her there, putting a few plants around the statue and a vigil light in front. We know that Mary doesn't need statues and pictures of herself, but we needed them to remind us of her presence with us. Our shrine was a good reminder of that.

As time went on, and our difficulties with our adoption grew, we found ourselves drawn to Mary more and more. Eventually we placed a picture of Brian and Andrea next to the statue and asked our friends to pray with us also. Each time we would begin to get fearful about their future, we would give them back to Mary and ask her to watch over them. She knew them before we did; she could be with them as we couldn't. She was their mother too. Then we would feel peaceful again for a while.

We drove Johnny to Colorado that last summer of his life. We were going to school at Regis College in Denver for six weeks and had invited him to come. He and his wife had separated and he was deeply depressed. "Bring your sleeping bag, your tent, your Bible and crucifix, and come and be with us. Take some time out from your life to get back in touch with the Lord and see what He wants you to do. Just come with us." So he joined us on our automobile trip from New York to Colorado.

Our first overnight stop was in Indiana at Notre Dame University, a place where we spent the first two years of our marriage, a place we have always considered as belonging to Mary in a special way. We went to the Grotto there shortly after we arrived and lit a candle. Once again we consecrated our son to Mary, asking her to watch over him, protect him, and heal him of his sorrow. We prayed together for a few more minutes and went on, forgetting we had even stopped there.

The night Johnny was killed, we called only the immediate family. It was very late by the time we were finished. The next morning we received a phone call from Kathy's brother, Dick, a Jesuit priest who was living in Massachusetts. Dick had been called the night before, so he knew, but that morning he had received a phone call from a friend who did not know of Johnny's death. The friend had had a very powerful dream he wanted to share with Dick. He thought the dream might have special significance but he wasn't sure exactly what it meant.

In his dream he saw the Blessed Mother. She was dressed all in white and was kneeling. In her arms she was holding a young man who appeared to be dead or asleep. She appeared much as she is in the statue of the Pietà. He recognized the young man as Johnny. Johnny woke up in Mary's arms. She smiled at him and he returned the smile. Together they stood up and turned to walk away hand-in-hand into a beautiful garden. As they started to leave together, Mary turned back and said, "Tell them he's all right. He's with me." Johnny was with Mary! When we heard about this dream we were immediately consoled and comforted.

About six weeks after Johnny's death, we were again at Notre Dame. Our daughter Anne was a student there, and we had gone out for Parents Weekend. The first thing we did was visit the Grotto. As soon as we arrived, we remembered our visit only a few months earlier. In our silent prayer to Mary we both said, "I thought I asked you to watch over that kid." Shortly afterward when we discussed our visit we learned that in the silence of our hearts Mary gave us both the same answer:

Her immediate response was, "I did."

Our reply was, "That's not what I meant."

It wasn't what we had in mind, yet it was. Mary was with Johnny throughout his life—and beyond. She was where we couldn't be. That's why we need her.

The statue of Mary we have in our home belonged to John's Grandmother Loftus. It had stood silently on a small homemade altar in her bedroom for more than fifty years. She got it from a church that was "modernizing" and clearing out some of their old statues (in 1900). When we first put our statue of Mary in the living room and created our family's shrine, the children were all teenagers. Their initial reaction was, "Good grief, now you have to genuflect before you walk into the living room." They weren't exactly thrilled. As time went on however, it became more and more a special place to go to think, to read, to pray, or to have a quiet talk with one another or a special friend.

When we returned to Colorado the summer after Johnny's death, Anne and Casey were at home. They knew we were dreading the trip and promised to pray for us. Each day we would check in by phone. They would ask how we were, and we would always say, "Fine." By the second week, the girls reported that they didn't believe us at all. They didn't think we sounded fine to them. So they put our picture next to Mary's statue, and they lit a candle for us. They placed us in her care until we came home.

We came to know Mary most powerfully as the Mother of Sorrows, Now a few years later, we also know other aspects of her. She is Our Lady of Peace, the Mother of Joy. Our family has new life these days. We have had three weddings. Casey married Larry, Anne married Christopher, and Brian married Linda. Andrea gave birth to Zachary a year ago and is a very fine mother. Both Casey and Anne are pregnant.

We are a close family. We see Casey and Anne very often since they live in town. Brian and Linda and Andrea and Zachary visit less often, but we are welcome in their homes, and they count themselves as part of the family. They are always here for the holidays. We love to have them.

God has been very good to us. Johnny's death caused us to re-evaluate many areas of our life. When the opportunity came to work full-time for the Pastoral and Matrimonial Renewal Center, we jumped at the chance. John left a tenured faculty position at the university in order to do so. There have been some financial sacrifices, but we no longer take our time on earth for granted. Johnny had twenty-one years to do his work for God. We decided that we might not live to retirement, or we might not have good health by then. We wanted to do whatever work we could, right now.

When we looked at the risks involved in moving from the secure job, we asked ourselves, "What is the worst thing that could happen if we leave the university to do this?" We decided that the worst scene would be that we would run out of money in a few years, the Center would close, and we might not be able to get another job for a while. We could lose everything we own. But what if someone came along and said, "Give me everything you have, and I will return your son to you." It would be no problem.

"Take it; give us Johnny." What is it all worth if our possessions cannot buy a life? They mean very little.

We believe that people who lose someone they love very much walk with one foot in heaven and one foot on earth. We have a strong desire to be in heaven. We have a lot of friends there. We don't have a desire to die, but we don't fear it either. In the meantime, we feel the presence of those already in heaven walking with us here on earth. It's a very comforting feeling. We have inner peace, thanks to Mary, Our Lady of Peace.

Our inner peace is actually the peace of Christ in us. Of all God's creatures, Mary was given the unique call to be the one to bring Jesus into the world. It is her cooperation with the Holy Spirit that brings Jesus to us, so it makes sense that we should turn to her in prayer as our intercessor for growth in inner peace.

14

Living in Peace

We spend our entire lives trying to be filled with inner peace. As finite mortal people, we will never be filled completely in this life. But we can constantly grow and have more each day. The same is true of healing; we are always on our way to becoming whole.

Sometimes we fear healing, believing that it won't work for us, or it's some form of hocus-pocus that is dangerous or no more than mind control. We offer a few general comments about healing, and then develop them a little bit in order to clarify what we mean by healing:

1. Not everyone experiences an emotional high from healing.
2. Healing and growing in peace are an on-going process.
3. There is frequently fear that the healing won't last.
4. Sometimes our problems seem insurmountable until we are healed.
5. We don't always have to reconcile in person with the one who hurt us.
6. Grief has a place.

Accepting Our Emotions

Inner healing can affect people in different ways. Some get very exuberant, light-hearted and want to jump up and down with joy and excitement about how good they feel. Others feel extremely calm, quiet and relaxed. They might prefer to be alone for a while to reflect on what has happened or is happening within. Still others are aware of having had a good experience, and they feel pleased but not ecstatic. Some have a rather tentative feeling. They believe something has begun but they're not sure. They feel a little better. Often these people have to return home to the person who hurt them or to a difficult situation. They're almost afraid to admit they are healed or get too excited. They dread being hurt again.

Our experience is that if we sincerely pray for the grace to forgive the one who hurt us, God does answer our prayer. Sometimes we're not entirely ready to let go of the hurt though. Sometimes it's still too fresh in our memory, or maybe it's so much a part of our identity that we're afraid to give it up completely. That's all right. God will only take us as far as we are able to go. If we wish to continue, it's helpful to continue to pray and search within for any additional barriers we may have. As they come to the surface, we can let them go. Little by little, God heals. Don't compare your emotional response to anyone else's.

Growing in Peace

We have seen many cases where the hurt which is the most obvious is not the deepest hurt. For example, a woman may want to be healed in her poor relationship with her husband. She doesn't know why, but she doesn't want to be close to him, even though he's a wonderful man. After her initial healing, she may realize there is another hurt beneath the first. Perhaps her husband reminds her of her father by whom she was deeply hurt when she was growing up.

We believe that God gently protects us from raising up some painful hurts which we are not ready to handle. We advise people to proceed slowly, seeking healing for what does come to the surface and they are ready to deal with. These might not be significant hurts in their judgment, but it is a beginning of the healing process. They can always move on to the deeper hurts in time.

Some people have not had any intensely traumatic things happen to them in their lives, so they're reluctant to ask for any healing at all.

J: *I can remember going to a healing service in which physical healing was offered. I had a severe sinus infection at the time, but when I saw all the people with cancer, diabetes, or serious heart problems, mine looked ridiculous in comparison. So I never asked for prayer for healing.*

We believe God wants us healed, no matter how slight or how major is our problem. Our hurts do affect the way we live and treat others. They color all our relationships and distort our vision, no matter how slightly.

It's important to experience healing even if it is for a small hurt. Then as an experienced healed person, you'll know that healing does work. You can continue to use the prayer process for more healing throughout your life and you can also bring healing to others.

Overcoming Our Fears

Many of us are skeptical. We don't really believe our healing will last. We're pretty sure it will just fade away by next Tuesday. Or else we believe that the minute we have to face the person/situation that caused our hurt, we'll be the same old wounded person again.

However when we read the scriptural accounts of Jesus' miracles, we don't doubt for a moment that the blind man's sight, the cripple's damaged legs, etc., were cured forever. We don't expect to see them on the streets again next week begging for alms. In the same way, when we are healed by the Body of Christ in our local parish, it is the same Jesus of Scripture who heals us. We might get hurt again by the same person/situation, but the old hurt is healed forever.

K: *After our initial healing experience in our hurt with Brian and Andrea I was very concerned that the healing wouldn't last. We were healed, but they weren't. How could anything be any different in our relationship? Sure enough, when we visited Andrea a week after the healing, she was in a terrible mood. She told us off and really let us have it. After forty-five minutes, we left. I was in tears.*

As we went out to our car, John was repeating through gritted teeth, "I am healed. I have been healed and I will remain healed." I didn't even bother with that. As far as I was concerned, this was it. I was healed, now I wasn't. I knew it wouldn't last!

At home that evening, I buried myself in the newspaper and TV programs. A few times John would ask me how I was doing, and I'd always reply, "I'm fine. Just bug off and leave me alone." The next morning, there was a similar response. When John came home from work that evening and got the same response again, he said, "We're going to pray." That night, we prayed again, and I was healed again. My first healing had not gone away. I was healed forever of that hurt. But I got a new hurt from Andrea and that is what needed healing.

If we have been hurt again by the same person, the only thing we have to forgive him or her for is the latest incident. We don't have to go back over the whole laundry list of the twenty-six other times this person hurt me. Just focus on the most recent event. We find that sometimes we need a few days to rant and rave, wave our arms around and be indignant and self-righteous before we're ready to be healed. But being angry and hostile just isn't worth it. The more accustomed we become to having peace and joy in our lives, the more quickly we realize that we need to pray for healing to restore it.

Overcoming Problems

Many healed people share that they realize in retrospect how they had made mountains out of the molehills in their lives. What looked like a monumental, insurmountable problem turned out in the new light of day to be not terribly important. As healed people they have a much calmer, reassured and confident outlook about how they will handle the real problems in their lives.

J: *I know this was true for me in my relationship with Andrea. While I was still hurting, I was defensive, seeking revenge, trying to prove I was right. I was super-sensitive to criticism (either implied or explicit) about my parenting. I was filled with self-pity and anxiety about how it would all turn out.*

After I was healed, I had inner peace and all the factors listed above were either significantly less intense or gone altogether. I was able to be part of the solution instead of part of the problem. Of course, the actual problem was still awaiting solution. It did not disappear just because I found inner peace. This is a noteworthy example of how the external situation had not changed at all but because of my interior change I could deal with it more effectively.

When we re-enter the real world, things *have* changed. We may have the same old situation at home, but *we* are different. We are much stronger. Our inner peace enables us to deal with these situations better than before. We also know we can use our healing process every time we need it and empty out all of the negative feelings and be filled with Jesus Christ.

We can also ask others to join us in prayer and fasting to ask that our enemy (i.e., the one who hurt us) will open his heart to God's grace and thus seek inner peace for himself. We are tempted to say we've lost hope with some people, but what we usually mean is that we don't *expect* that person to change. We must keep in mind Jesus' words, "For man it is impossible; but for God all things are possible." (Mt 19:26)

Here it is good to recall the meaning of Jesus' death and resurrection. The course of history for all women and men was radically changed by the single event of Jesus' raising Himself from the dead. Because of this He saved all of us from our sins and made it possible to break the chain of being hurt and then hurting others. He gave us the gift of hope—hope that we don't have to go on living as slaves to our past way of life. Each of us can open ourselves to His presence in us and through God's grace change our way of life and choose inner peace. All we have to do is take the first step, inviting God into our heart. He takes over from there.

Being Reconciled

Are we obliged to go to the one who hurt us and tell him that we forgive him? No. If it's possible, it's desirable. But it's not always a good idea. Sometimes the person isn't even aware we were hurt and telling him can cause more trouble. Perhaps the person is dead or 5,000 miles away or psychologically incapable of understanding us. Our prayer with the Body of Christ is sufficient.

We have had a number of situations where persons reported to us how those who hurt them suddenly called shortly after the healing. They're just checking in sometimes. At other times, the callers say they had a strong desire to mend their damaged relationship. Typically some time has passed since the last conversation, and those forgiven are unaware that forgiveness has taken place. But they will often say that they suddenly felt free to try to rebuild the relationship. When we forgive people we unbind them and allow them to be free. At the same time we gain our freedom and inner peace.

We also ask if we should go to those we have hurt and ask forgiveness for ourselves. Our experience has been that when reconciliation has taken place within the Body of Christ, including the Sacrament of Reconciliation, it is often sufficient. However our goal should be to carry out the scriptural call to go to those persons and reconcile if it's at all possible. If it's not possible, we can at least love in any way they will permit and keep them close in our prayers.

Accepting Grief

After a reasonably short interval after the death of a loved one, others expect and demand us to "get over it" and get on with life as usual. Perhaps this is because our grieving is such a deeply personal thing that they can't identify with it. But more likely it is because our cultural norms teach us to avoid all suffering. A grieving person is a visible symbol reminding others of the reality of suffering, and thus a socially unacceptable person to have around.

After Johnny's death Anne's classmates consoled her for a few weeks but then expected her to again be her normal happy self. When she was unable to do that, she found herself trying to "bottle-up" her grief so others wouldn't see it and then let it all come bursting out when she came home on a school holiday. As a result, she experienced a great deal of inner tension which caused her visits to be difficult experiences for all of us. Fortunately we have a close family friend who met with Anne and prayed with her for inner healing, something we had not been able to do alone.

In the months following Johnny's death we continued the normal activities of our family's life—visiting Anne at Notre Dame, going camping on Cape Cod, picnicking at our favorite parks, and celebrating birthdays and holidays, etc. Eventually it occurred to us that we repeated many visits to special places and many activities each year, almost like a family ritual. Our initial reaction was always a renewed awareness of our grief as the memories of our times together as a family overwhelmed us. Sometimes we thought that perhaps it would be easier for all of us to change our pattern of family activities in order to avoid our sadness.

The more we considered this, however, the more we realized how it was good, not bad, to keep alive our memories of Johnny. It is a parallel to the words in the consecration of our daily Mass, "Do this in memory of me."

This greatly altered our attitude about the meaning of grief. Up to that point we were looking forward to "getting over" our grief and returning to normal life. Then we learned that grief, in itself, is a normal, healthy response which helps us keep alive the memory of our son and keeps him present to us in a spiritual way which is much more total than ever possible in just a physical way. We accepted grief as a friend instead of as an enemy—a friend that will be with us forever.

We also learned that our emotional pains which were negatively affecting us were not due to grief but rather to our individual reactions to the grief. For John it was a fear of being out of control of his life. For Kathy it was a fear of the future and the additional suffering it would bring. Once we were healed of those self-induced hurts, we were able to accept living in peace with grief.

The purpose of healing is not just to make us feel better or selfishly bring inner peace to us as individuals. The purpose is to give evidence that God is present in the world and is involved in our lives. As healed people, we are all called to become apostles of healing—to proclaim the Kingdom of God. The simplest way to do that is to tell our families, close friends, fellow workers, and parishioners about our healings, and then invite them to join us in prayer for their own healing.

Final Notes

We have come full circle. As we look at the limiting conditions we impose on our lives, the commitments we make and the major decisions that hover over us, we see that more often than not we are constrained by fear. When we read Scripture, we see that one of the most repeated messages was, "Don't be afraid." When we take the leap in faith and trust God to love us totally as He says He does, we find ourselves living in love without fear in the Kingdom.

Love is our call and love is our purpose. How much easier it is to love when we are at peace within ourselves. Then we can love without any ulterior motive or the desire to win something back for ourselves. We can begin to love with the heart of Jesus and see others through the eyes of Jesus. As healed people, we have experienced the love of God, and, knowing His love, we have the same love for others.

When we are at peace, we can set aside fear. St. John tells us:

> God is love, and he who abides in love abides in God, and God in him. . . . Love has no room for fear; rather, perfect love casts out all fear. And since fear has to do with punishment, love is not yet perfect in one who is afraid. (1 Jn 4:16–18)

Most of us cloak our fear in nice sounding words so we can deny its presence. We call it "prudence" or "common sense." We say things like, "It's only common sense not to get too close to other people. I'll only be hurt someday when we have to part." Or, "Prudent people work hard and save their money for their old age. That way they'll never have to depend on anyone. They won't become a burden." In this way, we hide our fear of the future and our insecurities.

Pride can also be another aspect of fear. In our society, it's acceptable to be proud, so we avoid doing anything that will make us look foolish, weak, or different from others. Therefore, we avoid taking risks. We want to love and serve God in a total, all-out way, but our fear of the opinions of others prevents us from doing that. All of us are aware of the pressure of the peer group on teenagers, but the pressure of our own peers is equally powerful on us. Whether we are lay people, priests or sisters, we value the high regard of others.

So much of our daily lives is dominated by our fears that we tend to have pessimistic expectations for our future. Whether it is our financial security, our health, our job security, our lifestyle, our marriage, the moral and physical development of our children, etc., we imagine that many negative and painful consequences are in store for us. So we take even greater control of our lives today in order to protect ourselves from potential suffering tomorrow.

> **J**: *When we were about to adopt older children, many of our friends told us we were crazy to do that. They speculated that we would have both past environment and heredity working against us. "How can you do this to your older children?" they asked. "Don't you know you can destroy your family?" They were powerful words that made us wonder how foolish we were.*
>
> *Yet, as we look at our children today, we see their warmth toward others, their trust in God and their willingness to make and keep commitments, as a sign of their own growth and maturity. It's true that they have suffered. It's also true that they have wisdom and strength beyond their years. We believe that if we do good without worrying about the consequences, God will be with us and bless our efforts.*

Sometimes our own perfectionism hides our fears. We may never begin a project or make a commitment or share our inner selves with another because we don't know how it will all turn out.

We worry, "What if we fail? What if no one likes what we've done? What if it actually causes some harm?" We live, then, in a sort of paralysis—safe, yet discontent. We know that things can be better, but we will never do something about it.

Accepting our call to live in love may require us to change our lifestyle, our priorities and our values. If we accept Jesus' message fully, we may never be the same again. Yet, if we are fully alive, we should always be changing, just as the things of nature continue to change and be modified. Change is the essence of life. St. John says, "The man who does not love is among the living dead." (1 Jn 3:14)

Let's take a look at what love is to see how we're doing with it. We have chosen a passage from St. Paul's First Letter to the Corinthians and added a few statements to think about after each phrase. As you ask yourself the questions, focus on one other person in your life whom you are especially called to love. If you are married, it should be your spouse. If you are single, think of a significant family member, a child, a parent, a brother or sister. Those who live in community may examine how they love others in their community. Put a checkmark next to those statements you may need to focus on.

> Love is patient; love is kind. Love is not jealous, it does not put on airs, it is not snobbish. Love is never rude, it is not self-seeking, it is not prone to anger; neither does it brood over injuries. Love does not rejoice in what is wrong but rejoices with the truth. There is no limit to love's forbearance, to its trust, its hope, its power to endure. (1 Cor 13:4–7)

- **Love is patient** . . . "

______ I am willing to wait for you without complaining—even when you're late.

______ I enjoy sitting and listening to you talk.

______ I never nag you to change.

- **"Love is kind** . . . "

_______ I enjoy waiting on you and caring for you.

_______ I like to help you with your work.

_______ I bring you thoughtful little gifts or write love notes.

- **"Love is not jealous** . . . "

_______ I am proud of your accomplishments.

_______ I brag about you to my friends.

_______ I don't compete with you.

- **"Love does not put on airs** . . . "

_______ I don't see my ideas as superior to yours.

_______ I put you ahead of myself on my list of priorities.

_______ I take an interest in what is important to you.

- **"Love is not snobbish** . . . "

_______ I love your family as my own.

_______ I do not judge you by your education.

_______ I accept your friends.

- **"Love is never rude** . . . "

_______ I never call you names.

_______ I don't tell others of your negative qualities.

_______ Even when I'm angry, I'm gentle with you.

- **"Love is not self-seeking** . . . "

_______ I don't measure what I'm getting out of our relationship

_______ Spending time with you is more important to me than anything else I do.

_______ I share everything I earn with you.

- **"Love does not brood over injuries** . . . "

_______ I work through our disagreements right away.

_______ I don't pout, slam doors, or walk away from you.

_______ I find it easy to forgive you.

- **"Love does not rejoice in what is wrong** . . . "

_______ I want only good things for you.

_______ I don't plot to get even with you.

_______ When you are unhappy, I comfort you.

- **"Love rejoices with the truth** . . . "

_______ I am always willing to admit I was wrong.

_______ I never lie to you, even when it's "for your own good."

_______ I like to pray with you.

Love in action has been called a "harsh and dreadful thing," perhaps because when we decide to live in love, we no longer know what direction our lives will take. It is frightening, which is perhaps why we avoid total commitments and keep ourselves busy doing the many things that we hope will fulfill the commitments we have made. When we live in a loving relationship with God through our daily prayer, we are listening to Him. He does challenge us to some risky possibilities that we can either accept or refuse.

St. Joseph was a man who was always listening and ready to follow God . . .

> Suddenly the angel of the Lord appeared in a dream and said to him: "Joseph, son of David, have no fear about taking Mary as your wife. It is by the Holy Spirit that she has conceived this child. She is to have a son and you are to name him Jesus because he will save his people from their sins. All this happened to fulfill what the Lord had said through the prophet. . . . " (Mt 1:20–22)

The command was, "Do not be afraid." The proposal was to think about taking an action that was radical and counter-cultural. That's what we are proposing in this era of personal fulfillment. We are suggesting we need to die to ourselves; then we will find ourselves.

There is something in each of us that resists believing that our heavenly Father is an unconditionally loving God, overflowing with compassion and mercy. Jesus has promised us the Kingdom—a Kingdom built on His Father's love for us and our love for the Father. The Kingdom of God is within, and when we allow the Holy Spirit to be fully active in us, the fruits of the Spirit will be present. The fruits that St. Paul mentions in Galatians 5:22 are: Love, Joy, Peace, Patient Endurance, Kindness, Generosity, Faith, Mildness, and Chastity.

These are the fruits Jesus has promised to us and our families:

Love: This is an active outreach of caring and compassion for others. It involves listening, responding, the total involvement of one person with another. It is being life-giving in each interaction so that other persons become increasingly aware of their goodness.

Joy: The person with joy is a healed person. This person has the grace of forgiveness. He does not hold grudges against another. He is filled with enthusiasm and is optimistic about the outcome of all future events.

Peace: This is the gift of serenity and calmness. Even in the midst of turmoil and confusion, this person rolls with the punches, knowing that God will watch over her in all things.

Patient Endurance: This is perseverance. This person is willing to wait for results, and does not expect instant change in others. This person doesn't give up on someone, but continues asking God to answer his prayers.

Kindness: The person with kindness invests herself in others. She sees the goodness in another, even when no one else does. She is gentle and tender and probably would be good with animals and little children. She is adaptable and willing to change in order to please other family members.

Generosity: This person gives of himself. He is willing to sacrifice comfort and convenience to help someone. It's the person who can give up a favorite TV program or some private time in order to be available to others.

Faith: This person has a profound trust in God. She believes that Christ lives in each of us and brings out the Christ in others. Therefore, she has no need to control or manipulate people. This person can accept the mystery of suffering.

Mildness: This person uses no more authority or discipline than necessary, and does not over-react to situations. This person brings peace.

Chastity: People with this gift live their vows with joy and enthusiasm whatever their vocation. They show respect for the rights of others and practice self-control in all areas: use of chemical substances, diet, exercise, sexual activity, etc.

Whenever we become aware that we are behaving in a "non-fruitful" way, it is a signal that something is out of order in our lives. We need to take stock of our total lifestyle to see what we can change within ourselves. When we do this, we go beyond selfishness and egoism and "put on" Jesus Christ.

We believe that God wants to use us if we will only let Him. We believe He is present with us and walks closely by our side, whatever we may be doing. There is a purpose for our existence—a reason why each of us was born. Jesus spoke to us at the Last Supper in these words:

> Live on in me, as I do in you.
> No more than a branch can bear fruit of itself
> apart from the vine,
> can you bear fruit apart from me.
> I am the vine, you are the branches.
> He who lives in me and I in him
> will produce abundantly,
> for apart from me you can do nothing." (Jn 15:4–5)

Too often we cloud everything over and make life very complicated and difficult. Then we work very hard, trying to win God's favor, or we get angry and blame God for our difficulties. Yet, when we stop to think and pray, when we reflect on all Jesus told us, life is really meant to be simple. We only have to live in peace and "love in deed and in truth and not merely talk about it." (1 Jn 3:18)

The leap is in our hearts. We must begin within.